Cover illustration:
Gustave Fraipont, 1891. Digitally modified by Philip March.
Graphic courtesy of RKS Library of Drug Literature.

ABOUT THIS ILLUSTRATION

Gustave Fraipont (1849–1923) was a painter, sculptor, illustrator and poster-designer. This original graphic appeared on the back cover of *Le Livre des Fumeurs* by Spire Blondel (Paris: Henri Laurens, 1891). It was the last of 113 illustrations of tobacco, hashish, and opium including those in the pages ahead such as the frontispiece. The author and fictional narrator of the novel *Keef* were both users of these drugs and experienced hallucinations as represented in more than one drawing. The angel above was extracted from the background and adopted as the icon of RKS Library Editions.

Keef

Based on the novel *Keef. A Life-Story in Nine Phases*
by Timothy Wilfred Coakley.
Boston: Charles E. Brown & Co., 1897.

"Once upon a time of kif, a great story was told..."

by

Timothy Wilfred Coakley

A Story of Intoxication in Love & Death

*The Extra-Illustrated & Annotated Edition
of the 1897 Original*

**Introduction, Epilogue & Notes
By Ronald K. Siegel, PhD**

PROCESS

RKS LIBRARY EDITIONS

Keef

A Process Media Publication and Original Production of
RKS Library Editions

PROCESS MEDIA
1240 W. Sims Way, Suite 124
Port Townsend, WA 98368
processmedia.com

Printed in South Korea through Four Colour Print Group.

ISBN: 978-1-934170-70-0

DESIGNED BY PHILIP MARCH & RONALD K. SIEGEL

To Jane
My Scout In Morocco
Soul Mate Of My Dreams
Friend And Wife
This Book Is Lovingly Dedicated
By The Editor

The Magic of Dreams in the Desert[1]

---

1 *In Morocco never be surprised. If you see a donkey flying, just say Allah is capable of anything.*

—Moroccan saying

Men resting with a sebsi pipe of kif. Traditional Morocco pipes are made of almond or walnut wood for mixing Cannabis and tobacco. In closed or crowded areas camels have been known to act listless and behave oddly if not protected from escaping vapors. Yet the emptiness and impassive cruelty of the desert keep them together.

EPIGRAPHS

Moroccan kif-smokers like to speak of "two worlds," the one ruled by inexorable natural laws, and the other, the kif world, in which each person perceives "reality" according to the projections of his own essence, the state of consciousness in which the elements of the physical universe are automatically rearranged by Cannabis to suit the requirements of the individual....Thus, for a dedicated smoker, the passage to the "other world" is often a pilgrimage undertaken for the express purpose of oracular consultation.

Paul Bowles
American Expatriate Author Living in Tangier, Morocco

In the cause of keef and love

"My first experience of the witchery of keef delighted and gratified me beyond expression. I was satisfied that at last I had realized, in some measure, the dream with which I had solaced myself for months back; that I had found the long-sought key to the treasure-house of ideals. Without so much as a scruple as to its ultimate effect upon my physical and mental being, I surrendered myself to the alluring influence of the drug. The spell it wrought was essentially different from the effects obtained by use of any of the agencies with which I had hitherto experimented. In the condition induced by keef there was nothing of alcoholic fever, nothing of the gross gratification that opium-eaters know. So far from relating to animal delights, the pleasure experienced was distinctively moral. In the keef dream, the physical self was lulled into a state of unperturbed rest, while the higher mental faculties were stimulated to abnormal activity. The senses found Nirvana: the soul, enfranchisement. The zest that gratified ambition brings; the intoxication of the orator, buoyed up on a sea of plaudits; the divine delirium of the poet; the ecstasy of the great captain who hears the huzzas of his triumphant legions—these were the raptures which keef awarded to its votary."

Leon Abecassis, Fictional Narrator and Hero
From T.W. Coakley's KEEF, 1897

Happy Primates with Kif Pipe

QUOTABLE KIF QUOTES

"A pipe of kif before breakfast gives a man the strength of a hundred camels in the courtyard."
———Nchaioui Proverb[1]

"The classic story is the kif smoker's ability to outwit the drinker."
———told by Mohammed Mrabet

"In Morocco the dream-feeling envelopes one at every step."
———Edith Wharton, *In Morocco*, 1920.

"The kif world is where life is different."
———Paul Bowles

"Generally the kif-pipe is the means to attaining a state of communication not only with others, but above all with themselves."
———Paul Bowles

"Everything one does in life occurs in an express train racing toward death. To smoke [Cannabis, marijuana, opium] is to get out of the train while it is still moving. It is to concern oneself with something other than life or death."
———Jean Cocteau

"Time rushes toward us with its hospital tray of infinitely varied narcotics, even while it is preparing us for its inevitably fatal operation."
———Tennessee Williams

---

1 Moroccan kif parable, from the Riffan and Moghrebi traditions, is translated by Paul Bowles.

158. ALGÉRIE — Fumeur de Kif

Kif Streetwise Smoker in Algeria
During the Time of T.W. Coakley's Tour

CONTENTS

6103 SCÈNES ET TYPES. — La Mode au Désert.
" Kif-Kif Paris ". — LL.

"Kif-Kif Paris"
Camel with Protective Head Fashion for the Desert

FOREWORD
By Stephen J. Gertz

Upon its publication in 1897, reviews for *Keef* were extreme in their praise...

- "One of the most important publishing events. . .listed with Joseph Conrad's *Nigger of the Narcissus*, H.G. Wells' *The Invisible Man*, and Rudyard Kipling's *Captains Courageous*" (*Appleton's Annual Cyclopaedia & Register of Important Events of the Year 1897*)

- "A work of art exceedingly clever. . .pages betray a brilliant imagination. . .style is picturesque" (*Sacred Heart Review*)

...and condemnation:

- ". . .it is clumsy imitation, vulgar, sensuous, repulsive. To be objected to on all accounts" (*The Library World*, Vol. 28)

An obscure 119-year-old novel that inspires such broadly divergent opinion is worth revisiting, all the more so because the book is a rare example of the confluence of Oriental Romanticism and psychotropic drug use in American fiction.

Psychotropic drug use was not unknown to Americans. Two years prior to *Keef's* appearance, in 1895 Henry G. Cole's anonymously written *Confessions of an American Opium Eater, From Bondage to Freedom* was published (Boston: James H. Earle). "Heaven bless hashish, if its dreams end like this!" wrote Louisa May Alcott at the conclusion of her 1869 short story, *Perilous Play*. Eight years later in Alcott's *A Modern Mephistopheles*, a character uses hashish to enhance her singing voice, while another employs hashish to "violate the sanctity of the human soul." Louisa May Alcott was no stranger to psychotropic drug use. "To counteract the long-term breakdown in health she experienced after nursing in the Civil War, LMA became a regular user of narcotics, especially opiates and hashish, and other drugs," wrote Eiselein and Phillips in the *Louisa May Alcott Encyclopedia*.

If Alcott had known about keef she would have no doubt experimented with it. Keef (a.k.a. kif) is a refined product of Cannabis processed to heighten its THC content. Keef is super-hashish. And *Keef* is the first American novel to explore its use.

According to *Publisher's Weekly*, the top ten best-selling books of 1897 were:

1. *Quo Vadis* by Henryk Sienkiewicz.
2. *The Choir Invisible* by James Lane Allen.
3. *Soldiers of Fortune* by Richard Harding Davis.
4. *On the Face of the Waters* by Flora Annie Steel.
5. *Phroso* by Anthony Hope.
6. *The Christian* by Hall Caine.
7. *Margaret Ogilvy* by J.M. Barrie.
8. *Sentimental Tommy* by J.M. Barrie.
9. *Pursuit of the House-Boat* by John Kendrick Bangs.
10. *The Honorable Peter Stirling* by Paul Leicester Ford.

Aside from *Quo Vadis* and the Barries, they—along with *Keef*—have been nearly or completely forgotten.

Best-seller number 5, *Phroso*, written by Anthony Hope (whose *The Prisoner of Zenda* remains a classic) is a romance novel in the nineteenth-century sense: an adventure story. Moreover, it is set in Turkey. It thus falls into the genre of Oriental Romance, a category of literature wildly popular in the late eighteenth through late ninteenth-centuries due to its merger of adventure and the mysterious East; a winning combination to Westerners attracted to the exotic and, in particular, to inscrutable Asian mysticism, culture, and women, the object of Western male fantasies. *Keef* rapturously brings it to the United States. Returning from Tangiers to New York City, our protagonist—an artist—uses keef to summon the visions he feels are necessary to release and potentiate his creativity and allow his themes to become manifest in his paintings.

And what are those themes? Love and death. It is not surprising that a critic in 1897 would characterize *Keef* as "vulgar, sensuous, repulsive" because any undercurrent of eroticism would (forgive me) arouse the Puritan American mindset on such matters. In 2016, however, a book or film criticized as "vulgar, sensuous, and repulsive" would have no problem finding a ready audience, the words catnip to those seeking unconventional reading experiences outside of the conventional literary landscape.

And in 2016 no one would have a problem finding and smoking keef. As Dr. Siegel points out in his typically thorough manner, medical and recreational Cannabis can be found at your local dispensary with THC content equal to or exceeding that of keef.

The drug experience is based upon set and setting, that is, the mindset of the user and the user's physical surroundings when using. In 1897, a Westerner would have had preconceived notions about what they could expect from keef: wild fantasies expressed through hallucinations incorporating Eastern eroticism and the mystic. But no passé Oriental fantasies in 2016; we do not experience keef as nineteenth-century Americans did.

But with *Keef* we can. Lounge in your favorite reading spot, metaphysically (or otherwise) light up, and enjoy the product of Coakley's imagination and Dr. Siegel's comprehensive research.

SJG
Los Angeles
August 2016

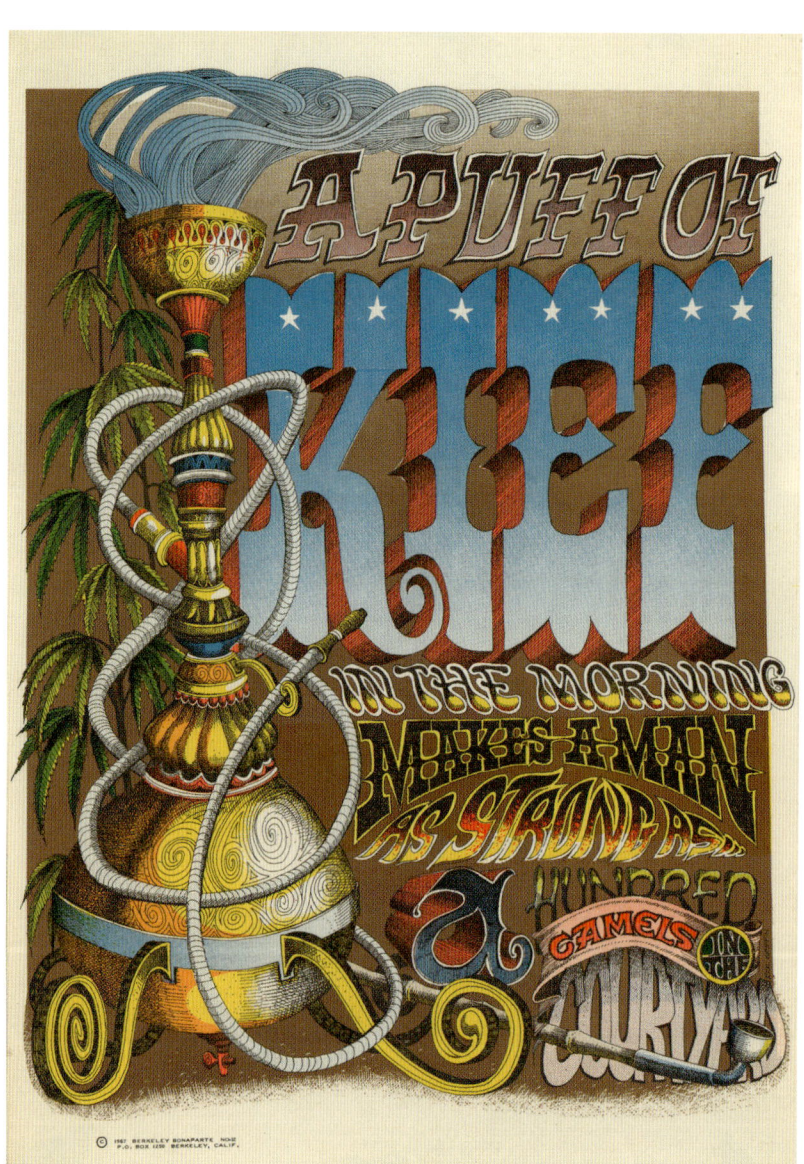

PREFACE

Weed of Witchery & Wisdom

The story you are about to read is based on an invisible cerebral reaction that occurs when parts of the Cannabis plant are used for their psychoactive properties. Among the native tribesmen in the Rif region of Morocco who have been smoking a Cannabis preparation known as kif (pronounced *Kē ef*) for over eight hundred years, it is accepted as part of the magic and sorcery in everyday life. This seemingly supernatural effect is neither physical nor psychological. Rather, it is an unconscious cognitive process involving perception, thinking and learning. It was first described in the Moroccan literature of the 1960s in novels and stories written by Mohammed Mrabet and translated by Paul Bowles. The cognitive process was given the name "Kif Wisdom." Since other preparations of hashish and marijuana can also produce this effect when equated for kif's potency, the more correct term is "Cannabis Wisdom" although kif remains the most reliable preparation.

The path to Cannabis Wisdom begins its slow growth as users share experiences of intoxications filled with a mix of dreams and reality. They begin to see day-to-day happenings differently and to think about the world in new ways. It is a world filled with rapidly changing mental images, even hallucinations, parading in one's head and morphing together with evolving thoughts as the mind's eye witnesses the creative poetry of Cannabis once glorified by Charles Baudelaire. The changing perspectives are often shared with fellow users who with a simple nod or smile acknowledge their understanding and acceptance of their own similar experiences. While there are individualized details that mix joy with unbidden feelings of sadness or fear and paranoia, there is a general acceptance of a truly meaningful experience. All a user has to do is to observe at a distance and avoid succumbing to stupor. In a sense the user is partaking not just in a shared joint but a shared worldview. The circle of users turns into larger movements that develop their own hippie or subculture language and stories, cause changes in culture, even religious beliefs and, yes, change history itself.

Cannabis Wisdom involves some consumption of Cannabis itself, usually kif, never forbidden in the Islamic moral codes. It draws heavily on memories, themes, and everyday conversations derived from being under the influence. The storyteller must then weave such experiences with characters, settings and plots that create meaning in a world which might otherwise reject the significance of kif or other Cannabis preparations. The best illustrations of this wisdom are found in the kif literature discussed in the following Introduction. The novel by T.W. Coakley was the first in this genre, appearing in the century before the work of other writers like Paul Bowles, Jean Genet, Mohammed Mrabet and Tennessee Williams.

In Coakley's novel *Keef*, written in the witchery style of an Edgar Allan Poe horror story, the narrator, a kif smoker, takes us through his supernatural search for love powered by his Kif Wisdom growing from his chronic smoking. At maturity, the wisdom allows him to see that the path to love goes beyond death. His novel, in the form of an illustrated memoir, was heralded as one of the most important publishing events of 1897. It made the list with H.G. Wells' *The Invisible Man* and Rudyard Kipling's *Captains Courageous*. Since average marijuana potency is now approaching kif levels (see *Editor's Note*), this book about toxic kif experiences may be the most important publishing event of today.

This edition is fully annotated with extra-illustrations. Furthermore, it is punctuated with endnotes explaining technical aspects, literary references, and elements from Coakley's life and travels where the story material was gathered. This "deconstruction" shows the origins of entire phrases, scenes, and plot points that were taken from previously published stories, then masterfully knitted together into a thriller that is hard to put down. The extra-illustrations bring the memoirs to life and show events happening as one reads along. After all, *Keef's* narrator is an artist and his illustrated descriptions presented on every page turn this novel into a pictorial opera of love and death that you will never forget. Yes, it's a trip you would be wise not to miss.

RKS

EDITOR'S NOTE:
ON KEEF, KIF, KIEF, KEF...

KEEF, The Word. You will not find the word in the *Oxford English Dictionary* but you will find several variations like "kief" that are pronounced the same (*Kē ef*).[1] *Keef* is derived from kef (*kāf* or *kayf*), Arabic for a state of dreamy intoxication further defined as delight, enjoyment, good humour, pleasure and well-being. The phonetically spelled *keef*, which is the easiest one to pronounce correctly, was introduced in 1808 when English travelers to Morocco discovered the habit of smoking a naturally occurring substance from Cannabis, the plant that brought us hashish and marijuana, in order to experience *kayf*, that state of dreamy intoxication promised by the dictionary. They spelled the Arabic word phonetically, thus giving us the English word *keef*. Still, the *kief* spelling is more accepted in English while the *kif* spelling is preferred in literary and scientific works. Nonetheless, confusion still exists among visitors when the classic Arabic words of greeting, *Kaif Halak* ("How are you?"), are pronounced, yet mistakenly heard as someone asking about the condition (*Halak*) of their keef. For the purposes of this work, the *kif* spelling is used to refer to the drug and the *Keef* spelling is used to refer to the original work by T.W. Coakley.

KIF, The Drug. Despite their shared botanical origins, kif is an entirely different drug than hashish in the same ways in which hashish is different from marijuana: preparation, potency and patterns of use. Different cultures have varying methods for preparing and using Cannabis but the active ingredients—chemicals known as cannabinoids—are the same in all of them. Yet concentrations of the psychoactive cannabinoids are different when different parts of the plant are used. Most preparations are designed for smoking or eating. Since bio-absorption is fastest via the lungs, effects can be detected within seconds while kif is smoked. Conversely

---

1 Variant spellings include kaiff, kef, keif, kief, keiff, ketama, kif, kiff and kiffer. Spellings in the Introduction vary with sources cited. The Rifains (early settlers of Morocco) named the plant *Ketama*, now the name of a village that has been a center of hashish growing and trading for over eight centuries.

absorption from the stomach is slower yet larger amounts can be ingested thus prolonging the effects. Marijuana usually refers to a green mixture of leaves, stems and seeds, parts of the plant that vary widely in potency. Marijuana preparations using only plant buds containing the potent resins can dramatically increase potency. Hashish is usually compressed preparations of the stalked resin glands from the unfertilized buds of the Cannabis plant. It appears as solid dark brown-black slabs and is usually smoked.

Kif is prepared only from the female flowering tops. They are harvested at seed maturity and dried. Preparing Moroccan kif "is an exacting labor, always undertaken by men of advanced age and experience. It consists of carefully cleaning the branches of the plant, separating the leaves and bracts from the shafts. The material is finely cut with a knife and sifted, recovering vegetable material [tan-blonde or "dirty gold" color and powder-like]...From time to time during the cutting activity, the knife is cleaned, removing the resin that adheres to it. According to the experienced men, this resin is considered toxic. Once this cutting phase of Cannabis material is completed, the preparation of tobacco that is added to the Cannabis proceeds."[2] Many kif users maintain that smoking kif without tobacco causes cerebral damage, leading to dementia and madness. The availability of Moroccan kif pipes, wooden sifter boxes, pocket grinders and other accessories found in tobacco stores give users tools worthy of a "sorcerer's apprentice" to turn homegrown or farmed Cannabis plants into high-potency kif preparations.

While high-potency preparations of either marijuana or hashish can be achieved, the preparations of kif are reliably the highest possible. Traditionally, owing to genetic variations and careful selection of resinous buds, the concentrations of THC (the principle mind-altering ingredient delta-9-tetrahydrocannabinol) are highest in preparations of Moroccan kif collected from the resin glands of the dried plants, hand-sifted once and then smoked. The preferred traditional route of administration is smoking in long-

2 Merzouki, Abderrahmane and Joaquin Molero Mesa. Concerning kif, a *Cannabis sativa* L. preparation smoked in the Rif mountains of northern Morocco. *Journal of Ethnopharmacology*, 81 (2002), 403–406. [Quote p. 404].

stemmed pipes with small clay bowls that hold tiny yet potent amounts. Throughout North Africa and the Orient kif, hashish, and tobacco have been smoked in pipes of various lengths as well as waterpipes with intricate designs. In Morocco, Turkey, France and other European countries, kif has been smoked in both tobacco cigarettes and cigarette tubes.

Analyses of samples collected from seized shipments have revealed a wide variation in the THC potency.[3] The results show distinct differences between the three forms of Cannabis: marijuana is lowest (average 3.39%; range 0.83–33.12%), followed by hashish (average 6.38%; range 1.0–50%). But kif samples show a much narrower range with consistently very high THC content averaging 26.5% (range 18.8–61.3%). The THC levels in samples of marijuana confiscated by police are now nearing the lower kif range (14%) due to improvements in cultivation. In certified tests reported by *High Times* in 2014 of samples representing the medical marijuana industry, genetic hybrid development, and private stocks, all were in the range of 22.64–28.35% THC. In 2016 testing of Cannabis Cup strains, kif-equivalent levels up to 32.13% THC were found.[4] Not only is it inevitable that such kif-equivalent preparations will become more common but the possibility of more toxic effects will become more likely with the growth of legalization and medical marijuana. Nonetheless, in worldwide interviews conducted with users, the difference between marijuana, hashish and kif was compared, respectively, to the difference between a beer, a glass of table wine, and a magnum of champagne from the finest vineyards. The dreamy intoxication of *kayf* is only a puff away, especially when smoking high-quality Moroccan or Algerian preparations. *Kayf* is also Arabic slang for café. A visit to a *kayf* where you can often find kif awaits you just around the corner in the novel that follows.

---

3 *NB*. Based on all tests for all years 1972–2008. *Microgram Bulletin*, 37(11), Nov. 2004, pp.197–198;University of Mississippi Marijuana Potency Monitoring Project (1972–2008); *Addiction*, 2008, *103*, 1100–1109; UN Commission on Narcotics, Drug Enforcement Administration, Street Drug Analyses, personal communications (2011-2016).

4 "Earth's Strongest Strains" by Nico Escondido. In *High Times*, May 2014, pp. 68–82; June 2015, pp. 69–84; June 2016, pp. 69–84. [All illustrated].

KEEF, The Book. *Keef*, a scarce nineteenth-century novel heralded as one of the most important publishing events of its time, is presented here in a new revised edition. As in other RKS Library Editions of lost and forgotten masterpieces of drug literature, every effort has been made to preserve the format and look of the original book while enhancing it with the deluxe addition of extra-illustrations, historical notes and annotations.

This novel was written by Timothy Wilfred Coakley and published in 1887 with eight original illustrations. The illustrations include seven black-and-white drawings sprinkled throughout the text and an inserted frontispiece depicting the novel's fictitious narrator. That frontispiece has been missing from many of the few surviving copies due to a poor quality glue binding. The World-Cat lists twenty-four surviving copies in libraries throughout the world. The book is available on microfilm in many more libraries and as poor quality e-books, most scanned from the copy held by the New York Public Library, a copy lacking the frontispiece and cover. All the original illustrations are credited to "Ritchie." While no other information was given in the book, the illustrations appear to be the work of G.W.H. Ritchie.

George Wistar Hodge Ritchie was a nineteenth-century New York etcher, printer, sketcher and artist. He lived and worked in New York City where he achieved acclaim from American artists, including Winslow Homer, who entrusted their etched plates to him. He helped organize a major Boston exhibition of original art in 1883 and illustrated a special limited edition of a romantic novel for a New York and Boston publisher in 1898. Interestingly, that book[5] by James Matthew Barrie, author of *Peter Pan*, was formatted in the same columns and fonts as *Keef*. Known best by his last name, Ritchie's sketches were either left unsigned or signed "G.W.H. Ritchie" on the bottom. He specialized in uncannily accurate sketches of people. Since *Keef* was printed by the S.J. Parkhill & Company in Boston, a company that printed books and illustrations for many publishers, it is likely they selected Ritchie,

5 Barrie, J.M. *The Little Minister*, The Kirriemuir Edition. Illustrated by G.W.H. Ritchie. New York and Boston: H.M. Caldwell Company, 1898.

a well-known New York printer and illustrator who worked on other books for Boston publishers. Many of his drawings bear a strong stylistic resemblance to those in *Keef,* thereby making for a worthy marriage of a master artist and a masterful novel.

In this new edition the text is reproduced in the same justified right columns as in the original 1897 edition. The book text here begins on a verso (left) page and runs continuously on verso with corresponding illustrations on the opposite recto (right) pages. All eight original Ritchie illustrations appear on verso pages following the same pages as in the original printing. All recto pages are reserved for the extra-illustrations (see following section). In order to provide space for these extra-illustrations the page size in the original 1897 book has been enlarged for this edition. The original justified columns (10.5cm x 6.5cm) were changed to a larger size (18.8cm x 11.0cm) that was befitting for the illustrations and twice as much text, thereby enhancing both the "show and tell" uninterrupted flow of the narrative.

The illustration at the end of *Keef* was listed as "Arabesque," a word that refers to a type of Islamic art design known for its complex serpentine nature. Arabesque patterns are often found in Moroccan rugs and depictions of flying or magic carpets. Coakley borrowed the word from Edgar Allan Poe who used it to indicate terror in a plot or character. In the center of the Arabesque is a kif pipe lying across a book, the same design found on the front cover of *Keef,* indicating that from cover to cover the book is filled with keef and terror.

Minor editing has been done on the text. Typos and spelling errors (e.g., "grewsome") have been corrected except for correct archaic British spellings that have been kept (e.g., centre, lustre, manoeuvre, or sombre). Also kept are new uses of words like "lightenings" that actually fit the sentence with newfound imagery rather than misspellings. Other words that work in this way include betrousered, literarians, Tangierines, and unfumbled, among several terms that are befitting the charming romantic and quasi-poetic style used by Coakley. Changes in grammar are minimal except where Coakley confuses "that" and "which" and where commas needed to be added. Conversely, excessive uses of commas that interrupt the narrative with unnecessary pauses have been trimmed.[6] Unnecessary hyphens in words that don't need them have been removed although a few are kept here in addition to archaic words and phrases in order to retain the original style of the writing during this period. Coakley spells several words phonetically and those spellings shared by other nineteenth-century writers, or in Coakley's other writings, are kept and identified in endnotes.

The Appendix is the usual collection of additional matter found at the end of a book. In humans, the appendix is a tube-like sac at the end of the large intestine that has no known function, but in herbivores and some mammals it helps the digestion of cellulose. The documents in this section provide additional information about *Keef*, the book, the author and the near-death effects of the drug. Taken together they will help both the reader and users of the herb alike to better digest the phenomenon known as Cannabis Wisdom as described in the Preface.

KEEF, The Extra-Illustrations. The term "extra-illustrated" refers to illustrations that have been added in this edition. Most of the extra-illustrations here were available in Coakley's time and refer to descriptions of people, places, works of art, and events found in the text of the novel itself. Many of them were available to Coakley and likely inspired details in his narrative. All extra-illustrations in the novel are captioned by their textual reference. Some illustrations in the novel may appear mysterious but are explained by the endnotes to the corresponding textual reference. Additional extra-illustrations in the Introduction, Editor's Epilogue and Appendix are captioned unless they are juxtaposed to an obvious textual reference. These illustrations refer to events surrounding the author and his life as well as the literary comparisons of *Keef* with other works of Coakley's time and those in the modern genre of Moroccan Kif Literature.

The process of locating images began with the intention to illustrate the characters, locations, objects, and works of art cited

---

6 Coakley, a political orator, utilized frequent commas to mark pauses in his written speeches, a style retained to some degree in his novel.

in the book. It started with the deconstruction of *Keef* and the gathering of textual descriptions by Coakley and corresponding drawings by Ritchie who was known for the accuracy of his portraits. During this hunt, and the concomitant research on the book's backstory, the search for illustrations produced over three thousand images that fit with Coakley's life and times as well as the story's fictional life and times. The final selection was based on artistic value and picture quality as well as considerations of page layout and printing. Most of these extra-illustrations display specific material elements (e.g., scenes from Tangiers and New York City, kif dens, rugs, etc.) while others reflect atmosphere and mood (e.g., cloudy kif dreams, reverie, love and death).

A number of recto pages do not have illustrations based on verso textual references. Instead, they display supplemental illustrations taken from pre-1897 references that were likely primary sources for Coakley's book and are inserted here to express the atmosphere of the nineteenth-century world of kif. They appear as black-and-white sketches or engravings without titles or captions. The images are framed by a kif-green border designed by Ritchie for another book by a Boston publisher that appeared the following year. These pictures might be found hanging on the walls of your house if you were reading *Keef* in 1897. Details about these supplemental images and their sources can be found in the List of Illustrations.

Twins. A few images were found to be nearly identical to both Coakley's descriptions and/or Ritchie's drawings. Since they were available to Coakley and Ritchie while the book was being created, they were likely inspirations for both the words and the drawings. The textual evidence is cited in the captions to the images. The visual evidence lies in the images themselves and is all too apparent when placed on the opposite pages of Ritchie's drawings of the major characters in the novel. For example, Abecassis, the narrator and painter shown in the *Keef* frontispiece and other illustrations, is smoking kif in "An Ambrosial Night" (page 74). On the opposite recto page is his slightly older twin doing the same in an illustration made famous and widely distributed during Coakley's time. Twins for the other characters are placed opposite their respective Ritchie drawings while details for all such selections are provided in the List of Illustrations. While Ritchie was known for the accuracy of his drawings, an important caveat is that these twins are neither identical nor fraternal but inspirational twins. In keeping with the phraseology of *Keef*, they may even be called Spirit Twins.

Two Ritchie illustrations have no twins that could be found among the approximately eight thousand photographs, cards, drawings, and art work that reflect similar but not exact illustrations of the times. The original Ritchie illustrations without a recognizable match are: "A Bottle and a Bird" (page 66) showing three gentlemen toasting glasses of alcohol, usually champagne or expensive wine poured from a dark bottle on the table; "The Unbidden Mourner" (page 124), showing a gentleman with an Abecassis beard and hair style, standing over a closed coffin in a funeral home. The recto illustrations show twin situations that occured in other illustrations with similiar arrays of people with the same action when explained by their captions.

*   *   *

Most images have been loaned by the RKS Library of Drug Literature, one of the largest private libraries of its kind in the world, and are used here with permission. Other permissions are cited in the List of Illustrations (pages from 186 to 193). Images without attribution are from unknown sources or by unknown artists. For example, the instrument player on pages 11 and 46 is from *Persian Designs* by M.C. Allen (1884) who describes the poetic sound as: "Like the faint exquisite music of a dream." Every effort has been made to trace accurate ownership of copyrighted visual material used in this book. Errors or omissions will be corrected in subsequent editions provided notification is sent to both the editor and publisher. These extra-illustrations, taken together with the annotations and endnotes, reveal the masterpiece that is this novel, once lost and forgotten, now found and unforgettable.

RKS

INTRODUCTION

By Ronald K. Siegel, PhD

Dream with me for a moment. Imagine that one of these nineteenth-century Bostonian gentlemen wrote *Keef* anonymously. Which one looks like the real storyteller: the husband of Elizabeth on the left or the husband of Virginia on the right? They look alike, share the same style of dress, and, as it will be shown, shared uncannily similar styles of writing. Accordingly, it could be argued that either one is the correct choice: Timothy Wilfred Coakley (left) or Edgar Allan Poe (right). The evidence of a strong underlying literary relationship between the two makes the choice difficult. However, if you know that Poe died in 1849, sixteen years before Coakley was born, you would have to believe that either Coakley discovered an unknown Poe manuscript, channeled Poe's words from some spiritual world, or in some other "inspired" way executed a masterful imitation of his style. Since it is precisely this spiritual dimension that can be visited with kif and will be explored in the novel, you may hold your opinion in abeyance now but revisit the possibilities after reading the book and the evidence presented in the endnotes that punctuate the text. Meanwhile, enjoy this unique literary adventure into the mind of a narrator/painter who, under the influence of the equivalent of today's most potent medical marijuana, seeks the love of his life... even in death.

Keef was Coakley's first and only novel. As such, he was following the rule adopted by many people writing a first novel: write what you know about and experience. Here it is helpful to examine the major events and experiences of his life that provided the raw material for the novel with particular emphasis on its theme of kif, and the romance "in the cause of keef and love."

Timothy Wilfred Coakley was born in Cambridge, Massachusetts, on May 10, 1865, just a few weeks after Abraham Lincoln was assassinated. As things were looking to his fighting Irish Catholic

Elizabeth's Husband   Virginia's Husband

parents, the Civil War was about to get worse. They feared for the fate of the large family they were planning despite the capture of Jefferson Davis on May 10. But on May 26 the last Confederate army surrendered and the war did end.

Their son Timothy, who was the third of seven children, went on to be educated in the Boston Latin School, America's oldest public school that produced five signers of the Declaration of Independence—although Benjamin Franklin didn't like the required Latin studies and dropped out. Here Coakley would have received a solid education in the classics. He then attended classes at the College of Notre Dame, Maryland, followed by graduation from the Boston College in 1884. At Boston College he won the prize for the best English essay and was selected as "class poet." Later, he studied fine arts at his alma mater that conferred on him the degree of Master of Arts. Like his narrator in *Keef*, he was a polyglot and able to use several languages.

After graduating, Coakley took up the study of law in the offices of two famous Boston lawyers: Hon. George H. Bruce and Hon. Charles T. Gallagher. In 1886 he was admitted to the bar but immediately went to work writing full-time for newspapers in Boston, and later in New York. He would not return to the practice of law until 1889, joining in a partnership with his younger brother Daniel H. Coakley. Together they handled civil and criminal cases including one high-profile murder trial from which Timothy inexplicably asked to be removed.

By this time Coakley had been writing for magazines as well as newspapers for several years. He also published a number of poems while gaining recognition as a good writer as well as a promising poet.[1] In 1893 he began to show political ambitions and participated in election campaigns at local, state and national—even presidential—levels. His attempts to win a Democratic seat in the State Senate failed but he continued to support other candidates in the role of "political speaker." He was often invited to speak on policy issues and in 1896 was invited to Chicago to lend his voice in an attack against the Gold Standard. After the Gold Standard was adopted he joined the Republican Party

---

1 See Appendix for Coakley's poems, pages 196ff.

Coakley at Boston College (Age 20)

and eventually worked for Theodore Roosevelt's election. It was during this period that he developed his skills as an orator and would eventually be invited to deliver major national orations. The most famous was the 1906 July 4 oration delivered at Faneuil Hall in Boston, a coveted honor previously awarded to John Hancock, John Quincy Adams, Oliver Wendell Holmes, and Henry Cabot Lodge, among other notable figures in American history. At the time, this July 4 Oration was considered equivalent in importance to a Presidential Inaugural Address.

In 1894 Timothy Wilfred Coakley was married in one of the largest society weddings that ever took place in St. Patrick's Church in Roxbury, Massachusetts. The bride was Elizabeth Josephine Smith, the daughter of a furniture dealer, ten years younger and from an even larger Irish family. *The Boston Daily Globe* published a feature article about the elaborate event and included a description of Elizabeth:

> The bride is a striking pretty girl of the brunette type, and is extremely popular in Roxbury society. She wore a gown of white duchess satin, trimmed with lace and the usual Tulle Veil, trimmed with a Lily-of-the-Valley pattern. She carried an ivory-covered prayer book studded with pearls. Her only ornament was a diamond pendant, the gift of the groom.[2]

The couple honeymooned in the South, and returned to reside in Brookline, an exclusive suburban area of Boston. It is reasonable to assume that the honeymoon glow continued over the next three years while Timothy was researching and writing *Keef* as suggested by his rather shy and cryptic dedication to Elizabeth.

In June 1897, the novel *Keef* was finally published. Coakley had written columns of newspaper stories and columns of poems so it was not unexpected that *Keef* would be printed in narrow columns, a traditional format for many small nineteenth-century novels. However, the printing of the table of contents on the cover decorated with a gold Islamic star and crescent was unique. His graduate education in art was evident in the story's references to

---

2 "Coakley-Smith. Wedding Was One of Brilliance and Largely Attended," *Boston Daily Globe*, February 6, 1894. [see Coakley Family Scrapbook, pages 202ff.].

Faneuil Hall

St. Patrick's Church

famous painters and their work. Benjamin Constant and Rudolph Ernst were among Coakley's favorites and the Oriental themes in their paintings, inspired by travel to Morocco in 1872 and 1885, respectively, provided colorful details that found their way into descriptions of events in this book. Coakley conveniently created a narrator who was a painter, a literary device copied from his favorite author, Edgar Allan Poe, that helped give him a voice for his artistic descriptions. Much of the story takes place in New York where Coakley had lived and worked for years. It was during this period that real hashish houses and Turkish smoking parlors were popular in New York and in other major cities, where they had been attracting crowds of customers since the early 1880s. Long-stemmed kif-pipes were often available in these houses and back rooms of tobacco shops. Turkish Pavilions at International Expositions in both Philadelphia and New York also provided smoking areas for sampling hashish water pipes. It is entirely possible that Coakley was directly exposed to details about kif or hashish smoking in such establishments thereby kindling his selection of kif as the subject of his story. Similarly, the book's detailed description of a Union Square tobacco store in New York with a kif smoking room in the back used by his narrator is an identical match to an actual famous Watertown, New York, tobacco store that is shown as one of the extra-illustrations. Newspapers and magazines were also running stories about the Empire of Morocco, its hashish trade, and illustrated the stories with drawings of Tangiers and its people, the city that became another major setting for the novel. And early books on hashish had just been published providing details and expressions about the experience that also found their way into his story. A major source was *The Hasheesh Eater* by American author and journalist Fitz Hugh Ludlow. Above all, Coakley's skills as a poet allowed him to grace the writing with beautiful poetic phrases such as "in the cause of keef and love" and "the witchery of keef." Throughout the book that follows there are illustrations and endnotes calling attention to these sources and further describing the fictional yet believable world Coakley has so masterfully created.

The publisher announced the novel with the following note that ran in several papers and magazines:

Favorite of Emir by
Jean-Joseph Benjamin-Constant, 1879

Smoking the Hookah by
Rudolf Ernst, c. 1885

New York Turkish Smoking Parlor, "New York's New Smoking Fad"
[*New York Herald*, Sunday April 28th, 1895, p. 10]

Charles E. Brown & Co. have just issued a romance entitled "Keefe [sic]: A Life Story in Nine Phases," by Timothy Wilfred Coakley, of the Boston Bar. It is the story of a Jewish painter, who in search for higher inspiration finds that the Oriental herb "keefe" [sic] gives him the exaltation for which he is pining. The form of a beautiful woman at last appears before his vision. And the story tells how he finds the original of his ideal and how her life is associated with his. It is cleverly written. Curiously enough, just about as the book was put on the market Mr. Coakley was called upon to give professional advice to a client who bore the name of Keefe [sic].[3]

Initial reviews were favorable, calling the book a "supernatural story," but none cited the obvious similarity to an Edgar Allan Poe tale. As a novel *Keef* was eventually listed as one of the most important publishing events of 1897.[4] Other novels that made the list that year included Joseph Conrad's *Nigger of the Narcissus*, H.G. Wells' *The Invisible Man*, and Rudyard Kipling's *Captains Courageous*.

Coakley's novel was written as a memoir told by a narrator who was chronically under the influence of kif, a powerful drug that Coakley called "the witching drug." It was the first, and remained the only, full-length novel devoted to the drug kif itself until the twentieth-century flowering of Moroccan kif literature (discussed below). Nonetheless, it remains a literary masterpiece.

In 1898, after helping in the Presidential campaign won by William McKinley, Coakley went to the Philippines on a mission for a law firm and stayed there for a year. His assignment was to negotiate the transfer of the Philippines from Spain to the United States. The newspapers correctly described his mission as "a trip of exploration to be converted into exploitation when he returns." Great things were expected from him and he succeeded in delivering the Philippines to Uncle Sam. When Coakley returned, he and Elizabeth settled in Los Angeles for several years. He joined the exclusive Jonathan Club and Sierra Madre Club, comparable to his memberships in the exclusive Boston Press Club and Irish Clover Club, as well as the Knights of Columbus. In 1900 he was

---

3 *The Bookseller and Newsman*, Vol. 14, p. 25.
4 *Appletons' Annual Cyclopaedia and Register of Important Events of the Year 1887*. Third Series, Vol. II. Whole Series, Vol. XXXVIII.

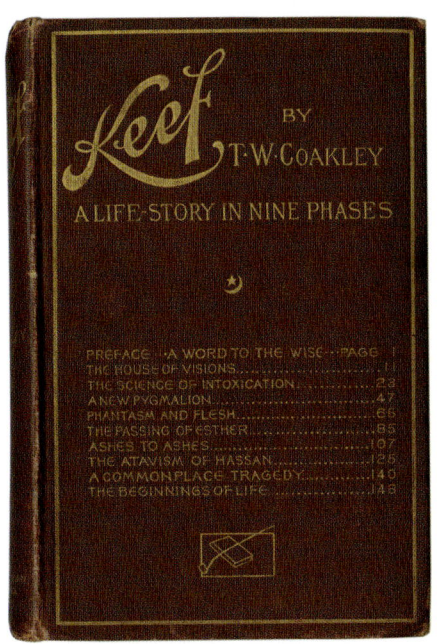

Coakley's Los Angeles house at 2525 Wilshire Boulevard where he spent winters on the West Coast since 1909 due to ill health including nervous breakdowns and physical handicaps. The house had ten rooms and three baths and as he suffered and died in 1914, so did the house, as it was demolished in 1934 and replaced by a Standard Oil station.

selected to deliver the Lincoln Day Oration in Los Angeles. Over the years, the Coakleys went back and forth to Boston with their Irish servant Margaret Whalen as late as 1910.[5]

Back in Boston Timothy had returned to his law practice with his brother Daniel. He became ill and had several "nervous breakdowns," a term used at that time to cover almost any manifestation of exhaustion. Timothy needed a long rest and decided to go abroad on the *Cunard Campania* with Elizabeth. When he applied for a passport (see Appendix), in lieu of providing photographs not required at that time, he described his distinguishing features:

> Age: 39
> Stature: 5 feet 9.5 inches
> Forehead: High
> Eyes: Blue
> Nose: Straight
> Mouth: Massive
> Chin: Round
> Hair: Black
> Complexion: Medium
> Face: Thin

The blue eyes help explain his fascination with blue eyes as manifested in descriptions of paintings and characters in *Keef*. The description of his mouth as "massive" was obviously a humorous reference to the massive moustache he wore. The Boston College photograph taken in his senior year at age 20 showed him without a moustache and with a normal-sized mouth. Nonetheless, he was a great orator, political speaker and lawyer so it must have been a loud mouth with a massive voice. That was the last description that remains of him and there are no further photographs showing how his appearance changed dramatically over the final years of his short life.

The Coakleys, along with Elizabeth's sister, Mary Margaret Smith, took the new *Cunard R.M.S. Campania* luxury steamship across the Atlantic for an extensive four-month tour of the British Islands, France, Germany, Italy, Switzerland, and Russia. (Coakley Family Scrapbook, p. 202ff.) It was a first-class ship with

---

5 United States Federal Census, 1910.

R.M.S. Campania

Drawing Room *R.M.S. Campania*

Smoking Room, Cunard Ship Line

elegant rooms that appealed to their society tastes (like first-class on a smaller model of the *Titanic*). The breakfast menu read like a buffet with everything from French plums to sirloin steak and Ceylon tea. They visited the "homeland" in Ireland and arrived in France at a time when hashish smoking parlors and opium dens were popular and would have surely attracted Timothy's interest. The group ended up in Algeria, neighboring Morocco, a setting for *Keef* that he had never visited. Algeria was flooded with their own equivalent of Moroccan kif, the potent variety that did not enter world markets. There were local cafés and sitting rooms where visitors could smoke the drug in traditional water pipes. It is likely that Timothy was tempted to go "next door" to Morocco, see Tangiers for himself and—pun intended—get the straight dope on those straight-stemmed kif-pipes or sabi.

The group returned home via stops in Naples and the Azores. They apparently enjoyed traveling and soon embarked on another extended tour through the southern states and then on to Cuba and Mexico. When they finally returned to Boston in 1904 they announced their arrival by inviting two hundred prominent friends to their lush home for a celebration of their tenth wedding anniversary that same week. Everyone congratulated Timothy on his restoration of health, a condition that would prove to be short-lived. Later in that year he was not listed in attendance at his brother Daniel's high society wedding where Elizabeth was matron of honor.[6]

Timothy Coakley continued with his law practice and political activity. He ran for Congress in 1908 but stopped campaigning after only a few days. In 1913 he was a candidate for the office of District Attorney but lost. Shortly thereafter he was arrested in a courthouse for unruly conduct and sent to the farm– actually the Pierce Farm, a Massachusetts State asylum where he was ordered to undergo examination by alienists. After doctors failed to find evidence of insanity he was released. Then he dropped out of sight, literally. One of the most picturesque figures in Boston vanished. He was suffering from a severe disease known as Erysipelas, an

---

6 The groom's mother was gravely ill and did not attend. It is possible that Timothy was at her hospital bedside.

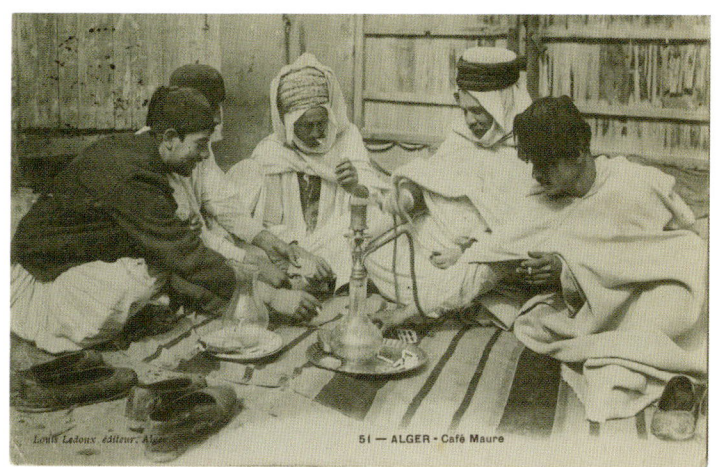

Algerian Hashish Café

A Turkish Sitting Room in Algeria

Woman Holding Kif Pipe in Hashish Café, Russian Empire

aggressive bacterial infection of the skin, turning it into horrible red lesions that appear on the extremities (arms, legs, hands, everywhere) but may occur on facial areas around the eyes, ears, and cheeks. It causes punishing pain that generates sensations of being burned alive, hence the Middle Age names of "Holy Fire" and "St. Anthony's Fire." Entire villages in France have been afflicted from an ergot-induced version of the disease resulting in unruly, panicked, and violent behavior. It can disappear for a while then recur again and again—a possible explanation of Coakley's unruly court behavior and frequent absences from public life—eventually progressing to necrotizing fasciitis (a.k.a. the "flesh-eating disease") that spreads to deeper tissue where it turns deadly. Coakley was given that diagnosis at the Boston City Hospital where he died on the frigid night of February 4, 1914. His last words were lost in a chilling scream. Since Coakley was active in organizing volunteers for militias and providing support for World War I, the hospital scene evoked the historic images of dead soldiers lying in their trenches with mouths and eyes frozen open. At the end, this promising novelist had become a frail and failing aristocrat hiding in a big house, surrounded by great works of art and expensive souvenirs from world travel, suffering a cruel death with a punishing pain that went on and on. He had turned into a character from one of the stories he always loved to read and whose author he emulated: the horror tales of Edgar Allan Poe. And, as you will soon read, it was not unlike what happens to a character he had created: Leon Abecassis, the painter narrator in *Keef*.

Keef is the first known English novel in a genre best described as Kif Literature. Other kif novels and stories appeared in the following century when expatriate American writers like Paul Bowles were attracted to the magic of Morocco and kif. They settled in the most bewitching city of Tangier (a.k.a. Tangiers) for long visits. Several early French and later English memoirs of travels in North Africa had mentioned the drug in passing, at times referring to it as Moroccan hashish but describing a product that is clearly kif. Others passing through stayed only long enough to sample the kif—sometimes unaware of its "magic." For example, Nick Flynn's memoirs of a 1986 trip to Morocco describes a grapefruit-

French Travelers in Tangiers Prison with Guard Smoking Kif

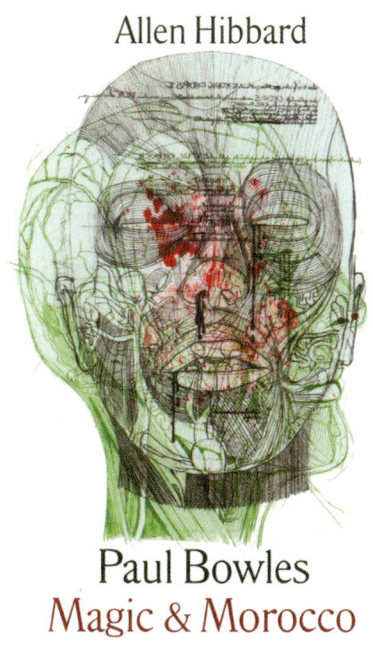

sized ball of bright-green pollen (called "unprocessed hashish" in the book) that he learns to make into cigarettes and smoke before getting out of bed in the morning:

> ....[kif] dulls and simultaneously focuses, reduces the day to a pin-point, to a voice inside laughing, a board strapped to your back to keep you standing—all you are now is high. Two joints and the doors close, you don't have to go out today.[7]

Coakley refers to kif with several telltale phrases such as "a won-der-working weed" and a "witching drug" that suggest he was fa-miliar with the literature of tobacco, marijuana, and hashish that frequently used "weed" and "witching" in their descriptions. In-deed, "weed" is almost synonymous with both tobacco and mari-juana. And "witching" has been used in both tobacco and hashish literature. In the 1889 temperance booklet *A Weed That Bewitches*,[8] tobacco is the evil culprit. In *The Hasheesh Eater*,[9] one of Coakley's sources, hashish is referred to as the "witch plant." While Coakley remains the only author to apply the "witching" word to kif and describe its effect as "witchcraft," the translated Arabic stories that form the foundation of modern kif literature (discussed below) use equivalent words, found in any thesaurus, to describe kif effects: "sorcery" and "magic."

Other novels that mention kif (either by name or as distin-guished from hashish in preparation, potency, use and effects) are found among crime, detective, and mystery books where the drug is mentioned in passing but is not a central theme. Sensational sto-ries and articles about the mysterious attraction and ravages of kif first appeared in French pulp magazines or books during the early 1900s. This was followed by a few English novels. In *The Laugh-ing Peril* an "oriental demon" attempts to destroy the entire white race by exercising hypnotic control after spreading kif (spelled kiff in the book and sometimes referred to as hemp) throughout the

---

7 Flynn, Nick. *Another Bullshit Night in Suck City*. New York: Norton, 2005, pp. 181–182. Inspired the 2012 film *Being Flynn* starring Robert DeNiro.
8 Talmage, T. De Witt. *A Weed That Bewitches*. New York: National Temper-ance Society and Publication House, 1889.
9 [Ludlow, Fitz Hugh]. *The Hasheesh Eater; Being Passages from the Life of a Pythagorean*. New York: Harper & Brothers, 1857.

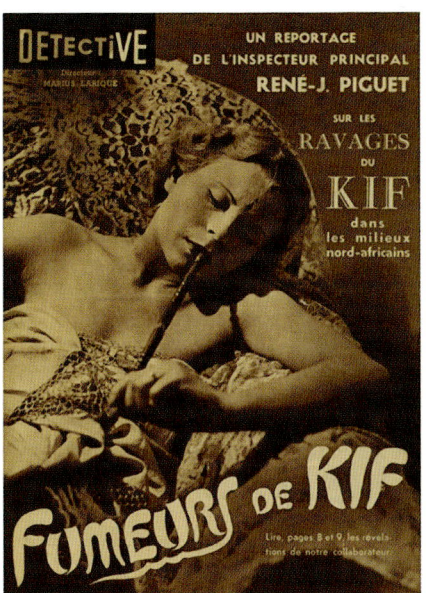

Kif Detective Story

Kif Mystery Hard Cover Novel

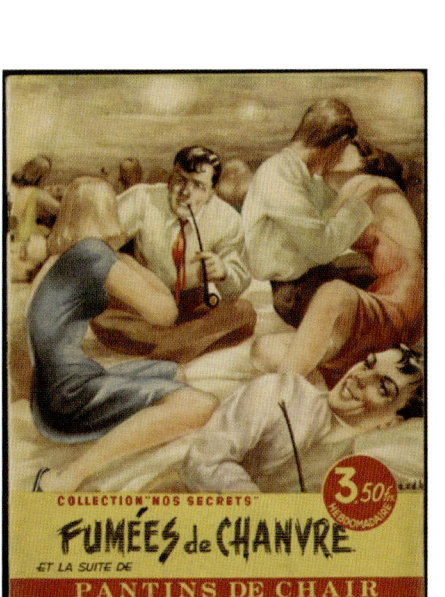

Kif Pulp Novel

entire world. Like novels of the mystery genre, Gates' kiff is used as just another narcotic, like opium, to seduce and control behavior.[10] These books reflect little information about the unique properties of the drug except its potency.

Here it is interesting to note that present-day kif growers in Morocco only sell their lower-quality kif (the second or third sifted batches of crushed leaves) in the world market because the best quality kif, that which is from the first sifted batch, would "blow your head open." The growers in both Morocco and Algeria reserve such potent kif for themselves and use tiny amounts with learned caution. They have been doing this for over eight hundred years. Deaths among browsing herbivorous animals have been reported and accidental deaths among chronic human users have been linked to confusional delirium and the secondary effects of hypothermia, malnutrition and dehydration.

The long historical use of kif in North Africa found its way into native folklore and stories transmitted as oral lore and cultural tradition. Since English translations were not available before 1897 it seems unlikely that Coakley had access to the material as most Moroccan literature was written and/or told in Arabic, Berber, or Moghrebi. He may have been equipped to read those few tales that appeared in Spanish (others in Italian) but no English translations were available. The Moroccan kif literature flowered in the twentieth century when Paul Bowles (1910–1999), an American expatriate author who, like Coakley's narrator, lived in Tangiers and not only wrote in English but translated other authors such as Mohammed Mrabet, perhaps the most prolific writer of kif stories.

Mrabet (born 1936) is the storyteller of the Ait Ouriaghei tribe in the prime kif-growing Rif region of Morocco. In his autobiography, he tells about his long history of kif use from childhood and adolescence on the streets of Tangier. Mrabet writes stories of the kif world "where life is different" and filled with hallucinations, magic and sorcery as part of daily living. It is a world where madness and superstition are as common as love and death. He emphasizes the role of kif by using the word *m'hashish* to describe a person whose behavior seems irrational or unexpected in such a

10 Gates, H.L. *The Laughing Peril*. New York: The Macaulay Company, 1933.

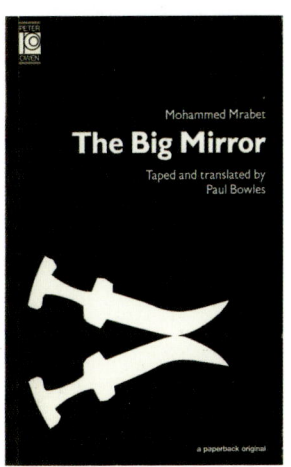

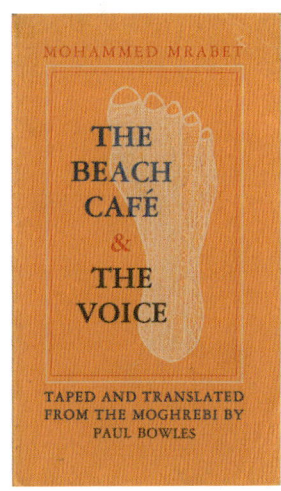

world.[11] Almost all of his stories and novels mention kif. In one collection there are tales of kif dreams, visions, violence, poisonous effects, and effects from mixtures with opium and tobacco.[12] Another collection[13] is based on a Moroccan folk-hero character, Hadidan Aharam, a country oaf who likes to smoke kif and, in fits reminiscent of reefer madness (a.k.a., "kif madness"), proceeds to chop off people's heads with an axe. Other stories reflect the joys of kif. In "Qrira" a man discovers that after smoking kif in a special pipe, the ashes turn into diamonds![14] In Mrabet's novel *The Lemon*, translated by Bowles, a precocious twelve-year-old boy grows up throughout the book coping with the intermittent use of kif as he struggles to keep his innocence.[15] Interestingly, one of Mrabet's stories tells about a kif-smoker named Hassan who likes his freedom. In Coakley's *Keef* we meet another Hassan who enjoys being a servant and dutifully prepares the kif-pipes for his master. There are many references to kif in Mrabet's other novels and stories and, even when not specifically mentioned, the underlying traditional use by the author and his characters reveal a "Kif Wisdom" that forms the *basso continuo* for the story themes.[16] A similar Keef Wisdom is at work in Coakley's pioneering novel as it confronts the modern world of love and death.

Mrabet has also written *Earth*, the only known play featuring kif.[17] It is a story about visions coming true and is told in the form of a one-act play with five scenes. The play is a classic example of the alleged magic associated with the power of kif, a drug that will not only "blow your head open" but the sky as well. Here we meet Jbel and Bhar who are smoking kif grown in special earth that Jbel has collected from a mountain forest. Bhar looks up at the sky

11 Mrabet, Mohammed (M.M.). *M'Hashish*. Taped and translated from Moghrebi by Paul Bowles, San Francisco: City Lights Books, 1969.

12 M.M. *The Boy Who Set The Fire*. Los Angeles: Black Sparrow Press, 1974.

13 M.M. *Harmless Poisons, Blameless Sins*. Santa Barbara: Black Sparrow, 1976.

14 M.M. In *The Chest*. Bolinas: Tombouctou, 1983

15 M.M. *The Lemon*. San Francisco: City Lights Books, 1992.

16 Chamdarlapaty, Raj. "In Defense of Tradition: Mohammed Mrabet's Postcolonial Leanings and The Confrontation of 'Kif Wisdom' With Modernity." *Storytelling, Self, and Society*, Vol. 3, No. 1, 2007, pp. 32–49.

17 In Mrabet, Mohammed. *The Chest*. Bolinas: Tombouctou, 1983, pp.81–98.

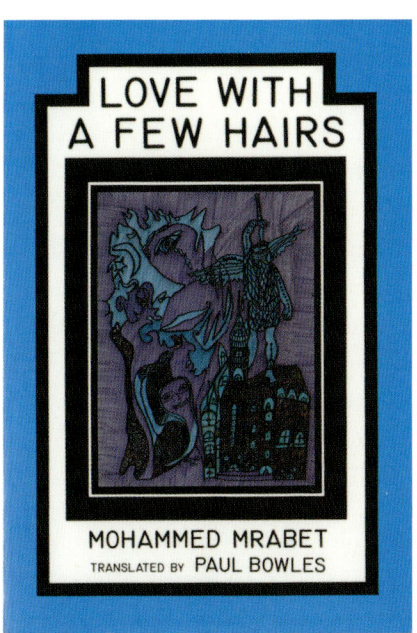

and has visions that convince him that kif will solve all problems. Jbel also smokes but can't see anything like what Bhar is describing. Their wives think they're both crazy. In Scene 2, a visitor is frightened when he hears the two men discussing their visions and is finally asked to leave. The wives are annoyed. The two men are willing to divorce their wives if they remain so displeased. Bhar continues smoking and describing his strange visions in Scene 3. By Scene 4 Jbel is finally describing his own strange visions while dinner guests are amused to hear about these extraordinary visions. Dinner is over in Scene 5 while Jbel and Bhar are now describing apocalyptic visions: the moon and stars are strange; a man wearing a turban is chasing people and animals, cutting them with a sword. Bhar goes to the window, stands and raises his arms to the sky. He yells: "Blood! Allah!" Then blood begins to rain upon him from above. His entire body is soon covered in blood. The guests are shocked and stand while staring with open mouths. Bhar turns to face them with his arms still raised, dripping blood as the curtain falls.

Paul Bowles, Mrabet's translator, wrote his own collection of stories based on kif intoxications including a story about one kif smoker who is swept away by his kif dream and begins to act it out in reality.[18] The same thing happens to Coakley's narrator, Leon Abecassis, who has kif dreams about his "spirit bride," the love of his life whom he pursues for the rest of his own.

Isabelle Eberhardt (1877–1904), was a nineteenth-century explorer, writer and kif smoker who traveled extensively in North Africa, writing about her contacts with kif and absinthe. She dressed as a man, converted to Islam and traveled freely in Arab society. Most of her work consisted of diaries and short stories written in French and none appeared until the following century. As a chronic kif smoker she undoubtedly knew what she was doing when she called other kif users "oblivion seekers." She writes about an encounter with such a group in a kif den on the road to Bechar, the capital of Algeria:

---

18 Bowles, Paul. *A Hundred Camels in the Courtyard.* San Francisco: City Lights Books, 1962.

Isabelle Eberhardt in North Africa

"The seekers of oblivion sing and clap their hands lazily; their dream-voices ring out into the night, in the dim light of the mica-paned lantern. Then little by little the voices fall, grow muffled, the words are slower. Finally the smokers are quiet, and merely stare at the flowers in ecstasy. They are epicureans, voluptuaries; perhaps they are sages. Even in the darkest purlieu of Morocco's underworld such men reach the magic horizon where they are free to build their dream-palaces of delight."[19]

Eberhardt was the most famous female kif smoker outside of nameless travelers and visitors who may have sampled the drug in nineteenth- and early twentieth-century cafés and smoking parlors. The most famous fictional female smoker was Helen Seferis, typical of the young girls known to have been abducted into harems. The erotic novel *Helen and Desire* tells the story of this young girl who is abducted into prostitution in Sydney and ends up in harems in Algiers where she abandons herself to the exotic hallucinations of kif.[20] After eating the kif in a traditional mixture with almonds and honey "her tent prison became an erotic kaleidoscope above her." Alexander Trocchi, a Scottish writer and life-long heroin addict, wrote the novel in a single week. The story was subsequently published in more than seventeen different editions in several languages, two sequels, with various titles (e.g., *Desire and Helen*, *Angela*, *Carnal Days of Helen Seferis*) and under either Trocchi's name or his female pseudonyms Frances Lengel or Jean Blanche[21]. In more than one edition, the reader is told on the book covers that the drug is hashish but the cigarettes Helen is always chain-smoking are later explained as stuffed with kif. In one sequel, *Return of Angela*, kif is prepared in cigarettes, or smoked in pipes, triggering wild sexual behavior—accompanied by equally wild adult writing that borders on the pornographic.

Throughout her sexual adventures Helen explores the sensual pleasures and weird ecstasies of her drug-induced experiences, an

19 Eberhardt, Isabelle. *The Oblivion Seekers*. Translated by Paul Bowles. San Francisco: City Lights Books, 1972, 1975, quotation from page 74.
20 Lengel, Francis [Alexander Trocchi]. *Helen and Desire*, Paris: Atlantic Library/Olympia Press, 1954.
21 Blanche, Jean [Alexander Trocchi]. *Return of Angela*. New York: Castle Books, 1956.

Front Cover

Back Cover

almost universal reaction to the "witchery of keef" that could help explain the perfervid romance generated by kif in Coakley's novel. While Coakley did not have access to this later kif literature, he had unlimited access to similar hashish literature in the libraries around Boston and New York. Sources available to him included memoirs, novels, poems, and sonnets. Even if you have read the 1897 edition of *Keef* or perhaps a print-on-demand copy, an entirely new adventure awaits you up ahead, just around the corner on the next page. It is a magic carpet ride into the world of kif, now in full color and with full disclosure of its makings as the pioneering novel of the genre. Imagine flying high over the green fields of "Morocco Cannabis" known as kif, beyond the peaks of the surrounding Rif mountains, and into the clouded twilight zone of a psychopharmacological romance. You will be guided through never-before-revealed events hiding behind the curtain of the text. Just follow the many numbered signposts in red italics-*1*-directing you to:

ENDNOTES

1 Read Past Them At Your "Laughing" Peril

At the end you may agree that what Mohammed Mrabet once wrote about kif also applies to Coakley's intoxicating *Keef*:

"This kif....It really hits you. It's beautiful."

Riding a Flying Carpet, by Viktor Vasnetsov, 1880

The Green Fields of Kif. Rif Mountains, Morocco.

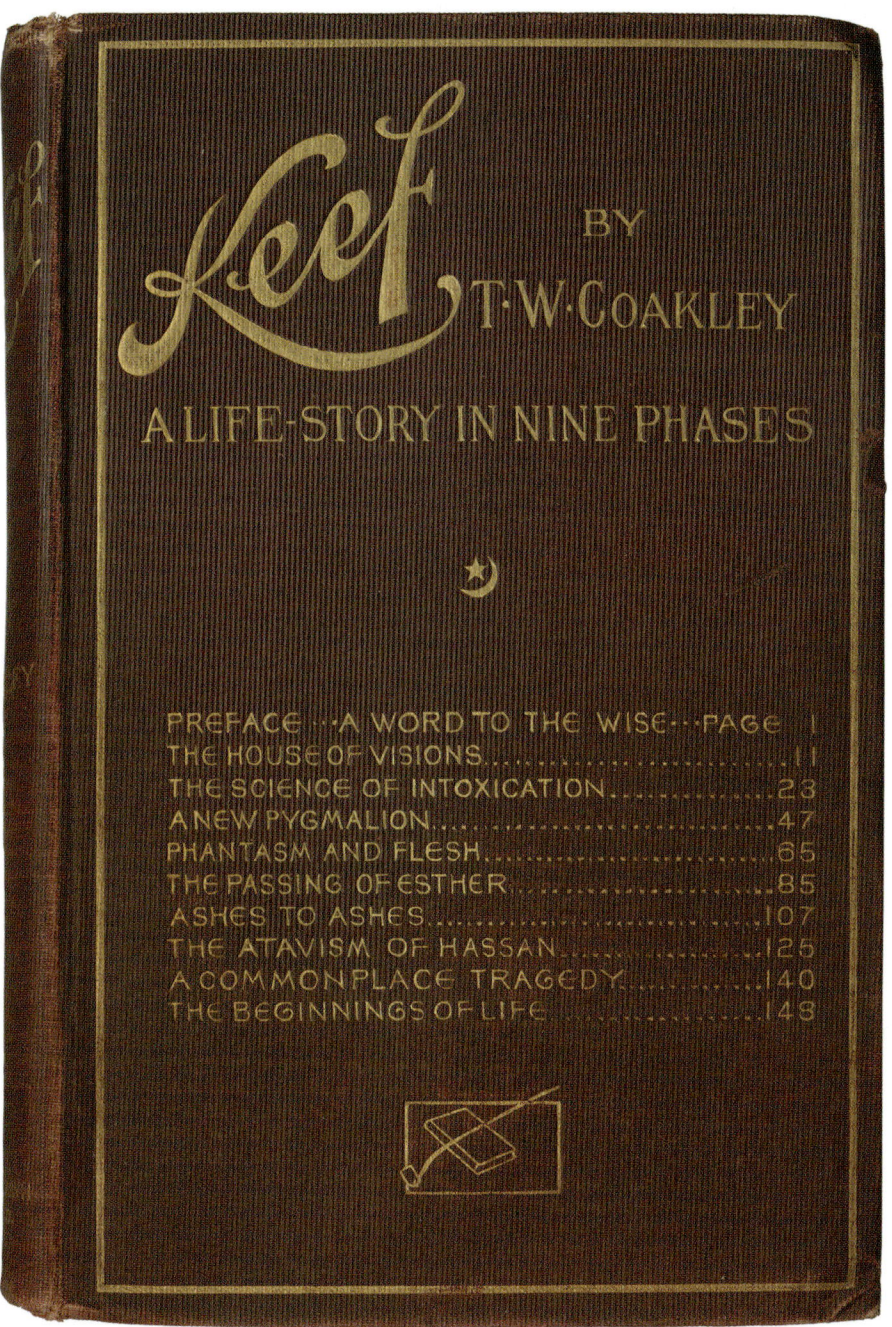

Keef

BY T·W·COAKLEY

A LIFE-STORY IN NINE PHASES

LEON ABECASSIS.

KEEF

A Life-Story in Nine Phases

BY

TIMOTHY WILFRED COAKLEY

With Illustrations by Ritchie

BOSTON
CHARLES E. BROWN & CO.
1897

Printed by

S. J. Parkhill & Co., Boston

To Her

who knows him best, yet loves him most,

this book is fondly dedicated

by the author

A WORD TO THE WISE

———

It is nearly a year since I came into possession of the subjoined memoirs.[1] The manuscript was accompanied by the following posthumous missive, dated and postmarked at Tangiers, Morocco:

MY DEAR CHALMERS: — When this reaches you, you will be the one man in all the world that knows aught of the history unfolded in the enclosed manuscript. With an important few of the details narrated therein you are already familiar. You have listened, with the intelligent sympathy that I counted on receiving from an occultist like yourself, while I rehearsed the story of my experiments and confided to you certain abnormal experiences, which it has been my good fortune to enjoy. Moreover, to you, and to you alone, of living men, it has been given to look upon the canvas, which the image of the radiant Esther transfigured and glorified. You were invited to view the opening scenes of a curious life drama. It is only fair that you should be informed of its consummation; and so I have set down the chronicle of my life, whiling away, thereby, many wearisome hours of a bodily illness that will soon be happily at an end. I beg you to make whatsoever use you may of the narrative; and, if you find it bald and crude in the telling, be good enough to remember that to the hand trained to wield the brush, the pen is, at best, but an awkward makeshift. I rest quite confident that our congenial selves will meet again, when and where, it were idle to discuss, for such a reunion can hardly come about until, for us, the fictions of time and space have ceased to exist. Until then, and ever thereafter, I am

Your friend,

LEON ABECASSIS

It is not necessary for me to give the circumstances of my first meeting with the painter, Abecassis. The history of our friendship is sufficiently treated in the memoirs that follow. Let me say, however, that he was the most fascinating character I have ever known. That he was a genius, no one who knew him doubted. His name, had he so willed it, might have been famous on the tongues of his fellowmen, for he had the sacred gift, which won renown for the masters of his art. Yet he lived serenely unknown, within hand's-reach of the honors he scorned to claim. Quite naturally, in relating a series of remarkable psychical experiences, Abecassis has omitted all mention of his personal appearance. This was so striking as to make him a marked man in any company. He was tall and slender, yet not lean. His form was moulded with exquisite delicacy, and his face was strangely, darkly beautiful. He wore a beard, but its short and silky growth served rather to accentuate than to conceal the shapely contour of his chin and the sensuous, yet clean-cut, lips. His eyes were black, large and brilliant as carbon. In conversation, he was incomparably impressive. Looking into the lustrous gloom of his great eyes, and listening to his finely modulated voice, one utterly forgot the speaker, in contemplating the ideas that he put forth. For one who lived so largely on idealistic lines, the painter had a curiously analytical mind, and much of the fascination that he exercised over his fellows was doubtless due to the peculiar coordination in his mentality of a lofty imagination with the rarest and subtlest reasoning powers.

In conclusion, I may say that while I failed to convert him to the beautiful and ennobling cult of Esoteric Buddhism, Abecassis was more or less imbued with the mysticism of the Orient. I may add that his nature was pre-eminently impressionable, sensitive and susceptible, in a remarkable degree, to all influences whether material or spiritual. I make this avowal thus frankly, at the outset, so that the captious reader may the more readily, by evolving matter-of-fact theories from this premise, explain away, to his own satisfaction, a tale that might otherwise startle him by its unconventional character. These prefatory notes are written and these memoirs published, not for him, but for that wise and sympathetic circle who believe with Abecassis that there are depths in life as yet unplumbed by science, and that only by careful introspection and the study of individual psychic experiences will the mystic veil be lifted that screens the kingdom of the spirit from the world of sense.

Respectfully,

EDGAR CHALMERS, THEOSOPHIST[2]

CONTENTS.

***

LIST OF ORIGINAL ILLUSTRATIONS.

KEEF.

—

PHASE I.

THE HOUSE OF VISIONS.[3]

I, ABECASSIS, Leon Abecassis, was born thirty years ago, in Tangiers, Morocco, the white-walled city on the cliffs that front Gibraltar. Were it pertinent to my present purpose, I might trace my ancestry to one of the most renowned of those Jewish scholars[4] whose genius and attainments made memorable the era of Moslem rule in Spain, and who, after the conquest of Granada, followed their Moorish patrons into African exile. But I desire rather to set down the experiences of my individual self than to rehearse the virtues which tradition has ascribed to my forefathers. At an early age I developed a passionate aptitude for painting, and this inclination was sedulously fostered by my father. I was his only child. My mother had died in giving me birth, and the lightest wish of her orphaned boy had become as law to the somber man of affairs. Perhaps, in encouraging my taste for art, he was cultivating, vicariously, and with a father's pride, an element in his own nature that had been all but uprooted by the sordid exigencies of trade. He had long since retired from active business, and occupied himself with the management of the fortune, which, in the natural course of things, was destined to be mine.

I got my first lessons in the use of the brush from an attaché of the Italian legation in Tangiers. The city of my home was rich in those gorgeous tints and picturesque bits of life that are as meat

Tanger-Maroc   Panorama Nord

2 Au Grand Paris, Nahon & Lassry, Tanger (Maroc)

"the white-walled city on the cliffs"

[Cavilla, Photo., Tangier.

ROOFS OF TANGIER FROM THE BRITISH CONSULATE, SHOWING FLAGSTAFFS OF FOREIGN LEGATIONS.

"the Italian legation in Tangiers"

and wine to the art student. In the universal carnival of color, I reveled as a flower revels in sunshine. I sketched everything in the town: the Bedouins, swart and gaunt, swathes in their flowing, white bournooses; the sleek, red-fezzed merchants, squatted in the bazaar; the frantic santos dancing in the streets; the groups of patient camels newly arrived from the desert with the spoils of the Soudan; the slave women standing with bared, ebon breasts in the mart where human flesh was bought and sold.[5] A subject to which I eagerly applied my boyish brush was a group of smokers, such as may be seen, to this day, in any of the resorts devoted to the sale of keef. Keef, it may be said, is a Moorish preparation of Indian hemp, and, in its essential principle, is identical with the hasheesh[6] of the Turks and the majoon of Calcutta. But while both hasheesh and majoon are used in the form of a paste or confection, prepared from the juices of the plant, keef consists of the leaves and tender parts of the plant itself. These are pulverized; and the fumes of the powders—which are frequently mixed with a mild and aromatic tobacco—are then inhaled into the lungs through the medium of tiny pipes of burnt clay. The practice had in it nothing attractive to me, aside from its picturesque features. What could I, buoyant-spirited youth that I was, know of the multifarious and potent forces which teach the jaded worldling the virtues of nepenthe[7] as infallibly as the babe's instinct impels it to suckle the mother's breast? Indeed, it never once occurred to me that these wan men I found drugging their memories with the fragrant narcotic were my weary fellows in the flesh, seeking respite from the sorrows of humanity. Rather, they seemed, to my youthful fancy, the unsubstantial personages of an Arabian night, or, if you will, a set of lay figures tricked out, in graceful guise, to gratify my whim and pose upon my canvas.

The resort that I visited was patronized by the moneyed class of Moors, and, not infrequently, a member of the European colony might be seen to enter its secluded portal. It was known in the city as the House of Visions. A sleepy-eyed Moor lounged eternally at the entrance and greeted all comers with the salutation in guttural Arabic: "*Bismillah*[8], blessed be keef!"

"red–fezzed merchants.... in the bazaar"

"groups of patient camels newly arrived from the desert"

"Bismillah, blessed be keef!"

Within, private stalls, luxuriously appointed, were provided for the unsocial few; and for the more companionable smokers one large apartment, furnished with sumptuous divans, sufficed. In this common room I used to sit for hours, leaving only when the fumes of the keef, involuntarily inhaled, warned me by a slight, feverish exhilaration to seek the air of the street.

I then invariably hastened to my little studio and transferred my impressions to canvas. I called my painting "The House of Visions," and, in my fond conceit, I thought it a masterpiece.[9] Even now, as I recall it, I fancy there was a crude realism in the work not wholly devoid of merit. I had faithfully depicted the familiar scene. The great, square room, its walls, draped with the brilliant tapestries of Fez, and studded with polished scimitars and shields; the turbaned and betrousered Moors dreaming on the divans, their forms dimly outlined in the twilight emitted by the single lantern pendent from the ceiling; the cloudy canopy of smoke, pierced here and there, by the starry glow of a blazing keef-pipe—these were the essential features of the picture.

On its completion, I fetched my father to my studio and proudly showed him my work. It was plain that the execution of the painting pleased him beyond measure, but he was surprised and pained by the theme. He praised my skill in a few, fond words, only to finish by exacting from me a promise that I should never again enter the House of Visions. I loved him too well to question his motive or dispute his bidding. The House of Visions knew me no more; and its mimic counterpart on my canvas was soon relegated to the moths and mould of the lumber-room. For the nonce,[10] the apparition of keef which, in crossing my boyhood's path, had so sorely perturbed my father, was laid. Neither he nor I could know that the spirit was fated to rise again and become the familiar of my manhood and the arbiter of my life.

.   .   .   .

"leaving... fumes of the keef... to seek the air of the street"

"The House of Visions"

"great, square room... Moors dreaming on the divans"

The current of my youth ran calmly on in the quaint, old, Moorish city. I spent my days, when not in the studio, in sketching along the coast, or in the rugged hills that skirt the town. My evenings were passed in the polyglot library, which my father had collated in his travels about the world. Like all Tangierines, I was something of a linguist.*11*   Spanish and Arabic I spoke from my babyhood, without distinction in facility; and my father had been at pains to school me in English, a language with which he had become familiar during a residence of many years in London, at a period before my birth. At the end of my eighteenth year, I betook myself to Rome, with a view to completing my education in art. I spent three years in the Eternal City, during which time I applied myself to copying the old masters,*12* under the immediate direction of the most famous painters of the day. I worked with unremitting devotion. My canvases were admired by my fellow students and praised by my tutors; but I had long since learned, in bitterness of soul, how weak and unworthy were my achievements beside the productions of genius. My first visit to the galleries of Rome served effectually to quench whatever spark of boyish vanity had found a lodgement in my breast. Several *dilettanti* whose acquaintance I made in the Bohemian circles of the city pretended to have discovered a budding genius in the person of my poor self, and urged me to put my canvases on the market. I laughed at them for their pains. I felt it in me to equal the petty performances of the day, but I scorned to enter into such a competition. The first canvas that I gave to the world as mine must needs be a work of real genius. I would leap to greatness at one bound, or, if climb I must, the ascent should be accomplished in the privacy of the closet. There, failure and progress alike would be screened from the unsympathetic stare of the multitude. And so I committed to the flames one after another of my productions, yet without losing heart. I determined to scour all Europe and, in the art collections of the capitals of the earth, to search unweariedly for the secret touch of greatness by which the antique masters had transfigured their canvases.

"I spent my days... in sketching along the coast"

Roma - Ponte Vittorio Emanuele II

"Rome... the Eternal City"

PHASE II.

THE SCIENCE OF INTOXICATION.

I was in this frame of mind when the unexpected and sudden death of my father recalled me to Tangiers. Henceforth, I was to be alone with my ambition. I conformed to the inevitable and tried to fancy that my bereavement was for the best. But Tangiers, after the funeral, was haunted by depressing memories and I was glad to get back to Europe and my art. I took with me on my tour, as personal attendant, my father's body-servant, Hassan, a Soudanese Negro of fabulous ugliness and gigantic stature, who loved me with the savage loyalty of a dog. In the course of the few years, I visited the chief cities of the Continent. I sought out the works of the masters in the public galleries and in the parlors of the *cognoscenti*. I fed my eyes to satiety on the luscious tints of Correggios, Veroneses and Titians without number. I gloated on the exquisite harmonies evoked by the magic pencil of Raffaele, the sculpturesque finish of Angelo's productions and the marvelous fidelity to nature of Rembrandt's lights and shadows. I studied the choicest products of every school, from the brilliant landscapes of the Flemish colorists to the gloomy grandeurs of the Spanish masters. But the farther I progressed, the higher became the standard that I set for myself. Advance as I might, my inordinate ambition still tantalized me. At times I fell into fits of dejection, which I terminated, not infrequently, by throwing aside palette and spatula and plunging into the frivolous gayeties of society, and the more questionable dissipations of the men about town. It was after one of these occasional departures from my usual orbit, that I crossed from Paris to London and busied myself with an inquiry into the peculiarities of the English school of art. I was not long in making the acquaintance of congenial spirits here, in the world's metropolis.

Among them was a man who, insomuch as he became my close companion and intimate friend, needs a few words of description. This was Edgar Chalmers, or, as he commonly styled himself, "Ed-

"I fed my eyes to satiety on the the luscious tints of Correggios, Veroneses"

"marvelous fidelity... of Rembrandt's lights and shadows"

gar Chalmers, Theosophist." A cultured gentleman was Chalmers, subdued and reserved in manner, and intensely imaginative. He was a devoted student of the Indian philosophies and a rapt and eager follower of Buddhistic dogma. He believed that he had a mission to prepare the Occident for the reception on Asia, back in the forgotten centuries, and he missed no opportunity of impressing his doctrines upon his friends. His temperament was spiritual to a fault, and his application to the Ramayana and the Bhagavad-Gita[13] intensified a disposition that was congenital. But while I disagreed with the views of life which this warm-hearted, blue-eyes American cherished, I could not stultify myself by deriding his conclusions. It was not for me, who had long since cut loose from the simple faith of my fathers and now stood dazed and dumb before the mystery of creation, to laugh at the solution with which he had stayed the questionings of his soul. There was a piquancy in his genial pessimism that charmed me. I delighted in listening to his naïve exposition of the beauties of "renunciation," the mystic influences of "karma," and the negative bliss of the "Nirvana" which, to him, was the highest good. At least he had the merit of being unconventional and sincere, and there was an ideality in his nature that strongly appealed to me. He had a loyal faith in my genius and courted my society. With many tastes in common and abundant leisure in which to gratify them it is not strange that we soon became chums.

When three months had slipped away and Chalmers was making ready to sail for his home in New York, I had become so much attached to him that the prospect of parting was not to be faced without a protest. Chalmers could not stay, to be sure. His presence was required in the American metropolis, where he was about to take editorial charge of a theosophical review. But there was nothing to prevent me from accompanying him across the Atlantic and making a visit to the New World. When I broached the idea to Chalmers, he was loud in his delight, and the upshot of the matter was that I engaged passage for the faithful Hassan and myself on the same steamer that was to bear my friend to his transatlantic home.

Arrived in New York, I found distraction and recreation to the full in studying the strange types and curious social conditions that

"the exquisite harmonies evoked by the magic pencil of Raphaele"

"the brilliant landscapes of the Flemish colorists..."

"... to the gloomy grandeurs of the Spanish masters"

are the natural outgrowth of a recent and cosmopolitan civilization. Temporarily I forgot the pleasures and pains of the aspiring painter, and gave myself up to camaraderie and Bohemianism. With Chalmers as sponsor, I met all the bright fellows whose wit enlivens the great dailies, and that more, more dignified coterie, the magazine men. I was initiated into the Siesta Club, an organization in which my friend was a leading spirit. It had a curious make-up, the Siesta Club, and the evolution of such a body would have been hardly possible in a city of the stereotyped and caste-bound Old World. Among its members were lawyers, physicians, stockbrokers, politicians of every party, journalists and literarians. Well-nigh all the races of Europe were represented on its membership roll, and, in many respects, it was typical of the composite life of New York. Good-fellowship was the sole test by which applicants for admission were tried, and any one with a veneer of good breeding was pretty sure to pass muster if he relished a bottle, a bird and a spicy saying. I found life at the Siesta a new and grateful experience.[14] The unconstrained exchange of sentiments and the unconventional mode of expression, which obtained in this Bohemian set, were a revelation to me. It was a relief to lay aside the buckram formality of European capitals, and, over a flask of mellow wine, to bare, for one brief hour, one's heart to one's fellow.

Indeed, the charms of the club were such that I should have soon become a fixture in its daily life, were it not that ambition, tugging at my heart strings, recalled me to my easel. I determined that, for the present, New York should be my home, and I cast about me for a suitable domicile, leasing finally an abandoned mansion in the outskirts of Central Park. This I fitted up with an Oriental pomp which gladdened the heart and kindled the black and listless eyes of Hassan, whom I installed as major-domo. I now gave myself up to painting with all my early ardor. From daybreak to dark, I toiled in my studio, indulging once again those golden hopes that lure the amateur to fancy himself a genius. Yet, I could not deny to myself my failure. While my productions were faultless in form and coloring, and artistically correct in conception, there was somehow lacking in them that divine suggestion of power that makes the

"the Siesta Club... typical of the composite life of New York..."

"...lawyers, physicians, stockbrokers, politicians of every party, journalists and literarians."

A Bottle and a Bird.

"the charms of the club were such that I should have soon become a fixture in its daily life, were it not that ambition, tugging at my heart strings, recalled me to my easel. I determined that, for the present, New York should be my home"

Editor's Note
The expression "A Bottle and a Bird" [see caption opposite page] dates to the period just before World War I (c. 1893) where late-night pleasures (e.g., a cold bottle of champagne) were sought out by young men-about-town in New York City. The bird referred to a woman of easy virtue (a hot bird). The expression became universal and men shared their pleasures. The skull on the mantel above forecasts the risks in war or peace.

paltry canvas live and speak along the centuries. I began to fear that I had fallen into the vulgar error of mistaking a lively appreciation of the beautiful and an abiding yearning after the ideal, for the possession of ideality. And still, I felt intimations of something within me that needed only opportunity and development to make of me an artist. There were evanescent moments when I felt myself inspired, and when a strengthening and informing element, which might have been the spirit of Angelo or Raffaele, filled me. Alas! So fleeting were these spasms of creative impulse that they were often gone before I had time to awaken from introspection, and, in every case, the inspiration fled before the detailed drudgery of execution. I was in a melancholy state of mind, indeed, when a saving thought occurred to me.

"If there were only some way"—I said to myself—"by which the transient exaltation of spirit which I have so often experienced could be sustained, then—ah, then—I might be the painter that I am not!"

Could it be possible that there was in nature some material agency that would accomplish the desired result? The experiment was worth trying, and I deliberately set at work to find a drug that would assist the operations of the creative imagination. It was a quest on which, probably, no man had ever wittingly entered. Myriads had given themselves over to narcotics and stimulants through inadvertence, discovering too late that they had fixed a habit, where they but sought to indulge a whim. The temptations to which they had succumbed I was about to court, and this, too, with the settled purpose and cool premeditation of an empiricist. I appreciated the risks which I ran in submitting a temperament so sensitive as mine to the action of powerful nervous irritants; but the stake for which I played was worth the hazard, and I had full faith in the strength of my recuperative faculties and in the sanity of my will.

In the privacy of my apartments, under the watchful care of the unquestioning Hassan, I started on a series of experiments that lasted for several months. I tried in turn, thoroughly, and under all sorts of physical conditions, the effects of alcohol, absinthe, cocaine and opium.[15] All to no purpose. Alcohol, used in light doses, was

The Watchful Guard by Benjamin Constant

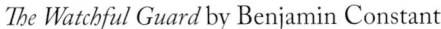

"under the watchful care of the unquestioning Hassan"

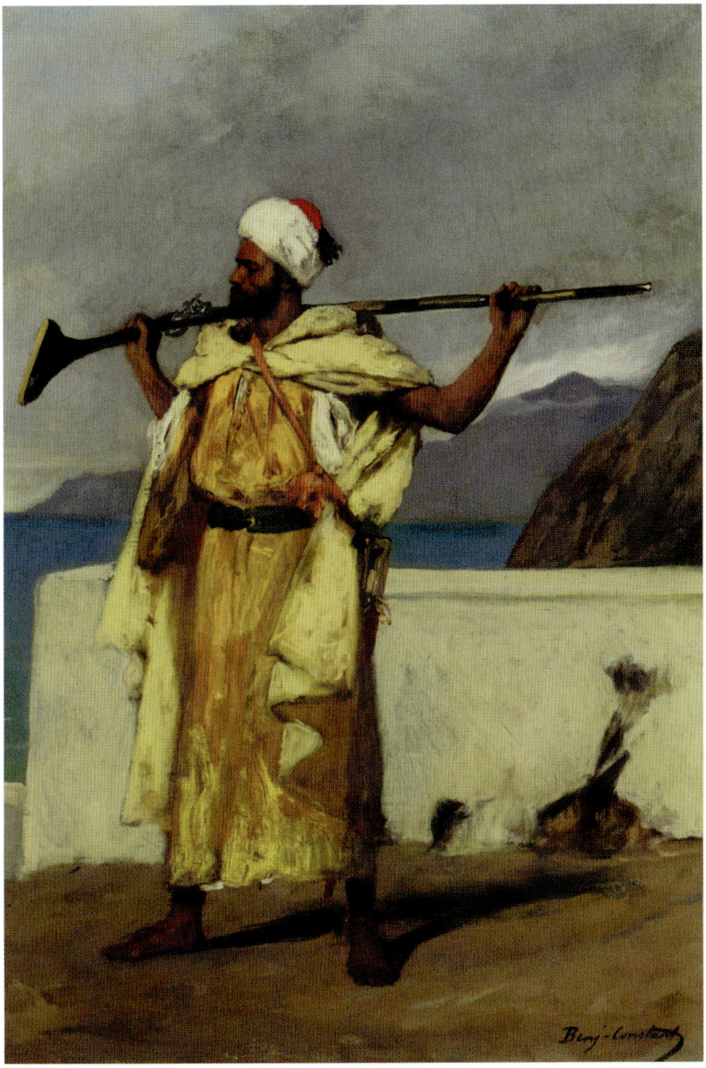

powerless to help me. When taken freely it produced exhilaration altogether too feverish to be valuable, and soon succeeded by uneasy delirium, with subsequent stupor. Absinthe and cocaine produced in me a kind of mental paralysis. Opium I used in various forms, and, for a time, I flattered myself that I had found the wonder-working agency for which I was searching. But this drug proved as disappointing as its fellows. I abandoned it when I had fully satisfied myself that its power was confined to the stimulation of the grosser elements of the imagination. I can understand how the metaphysical mind of the English opium-eater found in the drug a wealth of sensuous imagery that reinforced and illumined the severe beauties of his thought. But I needed no such stimulus. There was no lack of sensuousness in my tropical nature. What I sought to quicken and develop was the higher soul-faculty—the germ of spirituality that informs and vivifies every true work of art.

I had succeeded, not without a struggle, in escaping from the domination of the drugs, which I have enumerated, and I was about to dip into the pharmacopoeia with a view to experimenting still further, when a chance (or should I say a preordained?) happening altered the course of my investigations. One night, I drifted into a tobacconist's shop near Union Square. I was about to buy a package of cigarettes when I was struck by the strangely familiar look which the place bore. The shop consisted of one long room, the farther portion of which was veiled from view by a curtain of red fustian. As I entered, the drapery was thrust aside and a lean, sallow-faced fellow with Semitic features stepped behind the counter to wait on me. At the same moment a delicate, yet pungent, aroma saluted my nostrils and quickened my memory with the suggestive force peculiar to a familiar odor. It was the subtle and unmistakable incense of keef.[16]

This unexpected meeting with the Moorish drug filled me on the instant with new hope. Keef! The very thing! Why had I not thought of it long before? By reason, probably, of my long acquaintance with its use. Civilized man is prone to adopt the obvious and natural mode of procedure only after he has exhausted his ingenuity in following fruitlessly more recondite methods. I turned to the tobacconist, and addressed him unhesitatingly in the

"one long room, the farther portion of which was veiled from view by a curtain"

jargon of Arabic and Spanish that is the current speech in the streets of Tangiers. He replied in the same tongue and with the eager effusiveness of the exile who meets with a fellow country-man. His name, he told me, was Benatuil, a patronymic as well known to me as was mine to the tobacconist. The little world within the walls of Tangiers is not so wide but that a family name will be recognized by a son of "the Sacred City," even though he may fail to identify the man who bears it. Without loss of time, I communicated to my newfound acquaintance my desire to indulge in keef, and I was at once cordially invited to join him in a pipe. He led me into his retreat behind the turkey-red hangings, where I was duly presented to two compatriots who, like my host, were *tabaqueros*.

The nook in which I found myself was furnished faithfully in Moorish style, and with decorative effects that were quite surpris-ing in view of the commonplace character of its occupants. Huge shields of hammered brass shone flame-like on the tapestried walls. A massive bronze lantern, suspended by a brazen chain, dangled from the ceilings. Rugs of picturesque patterns, though coarse in fabric, littered the floor, and here and there were ottomans covered with a mosaic of stained leather. In the centre of the room stood a table, lying on which were several reed-stemmed pipes of red clay. There, too, heaped in the middle of the board and gleaming duskily in the lantern light, with the metallic lustre of a miser's treasure, lay a quantity of Indian hemp. One of my host's visitors was indolently stripping the yellow-green leaves from their parent twigs and powdering them between his brown palms. His com-panion puffed at a keef-pipe with tranquil complacency, stopping now and then to mix the powdered herb with portions of fine-cut Havana leaf. A pack of well-thumbed *naipes*, the playing cards of the Spanish, stared, face upward, from the table.

I had been so long severed in spirit, as well as body, from the old life of Tangiers that this recurrence to the scenes of my dreamy boyhood was a rich treat for me; and when my host brought forth from some mysterious recess a pot of steaming, black coffee, I was only too ready to throw myself on an ottoman and join in the feast. It may have been due to my haphazard contact with an en-

"The nook...was furnished faithfully in Moorish style...."

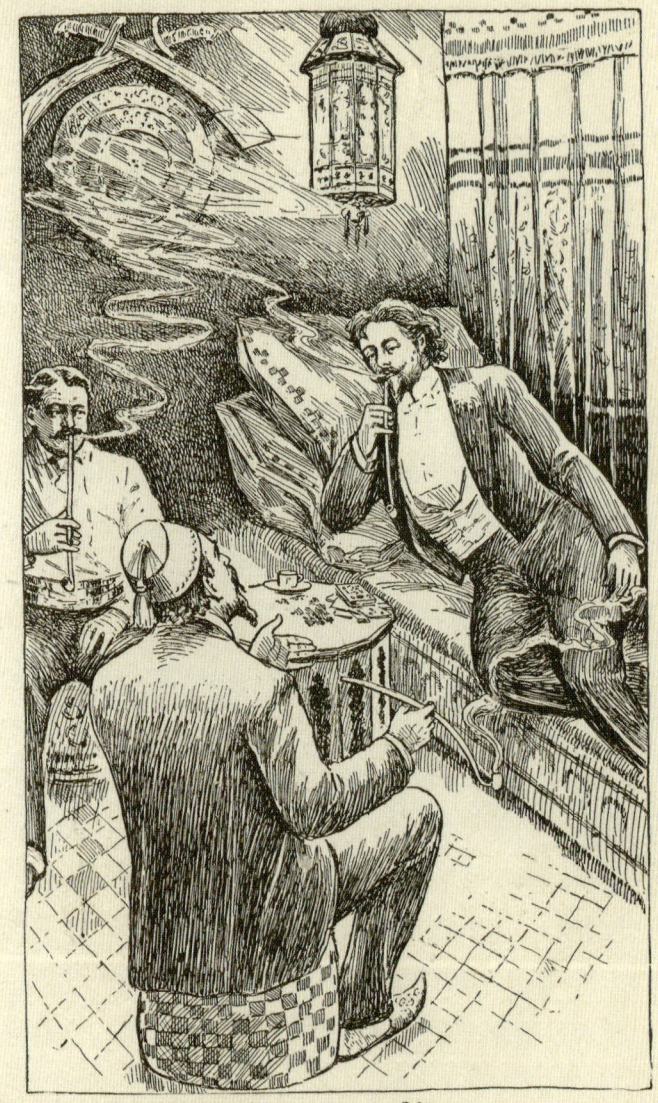

AN AMBROSIAL NIGHT.

"His companion puffed at a keef-pipe with tranquil complacency"

vironment which renewed the memories of my youth; it may have been due to the subtle influence of the keef fumes, unconsciously inhaled; but, to whatsoever the effect may be attributed, I felt that I was about to enter a new sphere of existence. I eyed Benatuil intently as he proceeded, with solemn Eastern courtesy, to prepare a pipe with its fragrant charge; and I could not have experienced a greater awe if he were some mighty hypnotist, working a spell with which to snare my soul. I remember strangely, and as one remembers a long-gone, sweet experience, the succeeding happenings of that night. I know that there passed a period of lazy contemplation. We chatted of Tangiers, and I saw its tangled streets and sunlit walls in the azure clouds, which I blew from my first keef-pipe. I smoked immoderately, and my mood merged, after a while, into one of divine merriment. My matter-of-fact associates disclosed to me the most heroic qualities. Their gossip was the loftiest sentiment, their dull badinage the sublimest wit. Their mirth was as the laughter of the gods. I could not but share in it and count myself an Olympian, too.

I remember—not indistinctly, yet remotely—seeking my bachelor home and threading my way through the streets of the great city with a rare sense of exaltation and in a mood which lent to the meanest of objects a regal grace, an ideal charm. The town to me was a metropolis of fairyland. The electric stars, which glittered along the prosaic thoroughfare, I knew at sight for the elemental lightnings harnessed by the genius of humanity. I looked on the great building, towering dizzily skyward, and learned that mortal man, as in the olden myth, still labors to scale high heaven. Here was a romance of architecture fresher and truer than that which clothes ancestral palaces, mosques and castellated piles. The horseless car shamed the triumphal chariot of Caesar. The work-a-day mob of passers-by were my brothers now—a radiant company of immortals; and the wan and shriveled sandwich-man who jostled me, as he went by, was no shabby toiler of the slums, but a noble spirit in whose fact I read the record of a tragic duel with fate. Arrived at my rooms, I yielded to the insistent influence of the drug and fell into a fitful slumber, interspersed with the glory of great thoughts and cheerful sentiments. Then came a period of vague

"I saw its tangled streets..."

"...and sunlit walls in the azure clouds"

"The electric stars, which glittered along the prosaic thoroughfare..."

suggestion, an uplifting of the heart, a panting after the sweet waters of the fountains of the ideal and the unknown, an undefined attraction towards some mysterious affinity, a period when I felt and knew that there was some puissant entity seeking to reach and act upon my life. And while seeking to fathom the problem, I was environed by distracting dreams and beguiled into oblivion.

"I was environed by distracting dreams and beguiled into oblivion"

PHASE III.

A NEW PYGMALION.

MY first experience of the witchery[17] of keef delighted and gratified me beyond expression. I was satisfied that at last I had realized, in some measure, the dream with which I had solaced myself for months back; that I had found the long-sought key to the
treasure-house of ideals. Without so much as a scruple as to its
ultimate effect upon my physical and mental being, I surrendered
myself to the alluring influence of the drug. The spell it wrought
was essentially different from the effects obtained by use of any
of the agencies with which I had hitherto experimented. In the
condition induced by keef there was nothing of alcoholic fever,
nothing of the gross gratification that opium-eaters know. So far
from relating to animal delights, the pleasure experienced was distinctively moral. In the keef dream, the physical self was lulled
into a state of unperturbed rest, while the higher mental faculties
were stimulated to abnormal activity. The senses found Nirvana:
the soul, enfranchisement. The zest that gratified ambition brings;
the intoxication of the orator, buoyed up on a sea of plaudits;[18] the
divine delirium of the poet; the ecstasy of the great captain who
hears the huzzas of his triumphant legions—these were the raptures which keef awarded to its votary.

On the day following my first keef dream, I visited Benatuil's
and procured a store of the drug, for I found myself already long-
ing to smoke with uncontrollable desire.[19] To be sure, I had not
as yet the acquired appetite which enslaves[20] the habitual smoker,
but I had a no less potent motive in the belief that the drug was
an instrument through which I could stimulate my imagination
to such an extent as to realize on canvas the visions which had
been dimly and momentarily foreshadowed to my spirit. I was not
long in discovering that the mystic effect of the drug was marked
by three successive stages, which could be differentiated from one
another without difficulty.

The first stage was a languorous reverie, in which all material
cares were eliminated from life, and the mind, freed from the tasks

"higher mental faculties were stimulated to abnormal activity"

and distractions of the sordid world, floated calmly and repose-fully along pleasing channels of thought. As the drug gained in power, this phase was followed by that of fantasy. Here the mind took note of the phenomena of the physical universe with a truer and subtler apprehension than normally. The percipient discov-ered something of the beautiful in all things, interpreted nature and art alike with unfailing cheerfulness and grasped instinctively the dignity of life and all the finer joys and truths of existence. Finally, there came the exaltation of spirit to which I have already alluded and which undoubtedly constituted the chief charm of the drug. This was a state in which the mind seemed, for the nonce, in full accord with the infinite, in which time and space, pain and remorse, misgiving and satiety were blotted out in one, supreme, ecstatic sense of being.[21] This culminating stage was succeeded, all too quickly, by a coma-like sleep.

In due time, I learned that the phenomena, both in the state of fantasy and in that of ecstasy, were perceptibly affected by the mood in which I found myself when setting out to smoke. This was so true that I studied to put myself in a responsive frame of mind, and on a high plane of thought, before wooing the drug. I usually sought the pipe after protracted meditations upon high philosophies, or when fresh from poring over the splendid pages of the world's great poets. In this way I found that by saturating my imagination with a drama of Shakespeare's or Calderon's, a lyric of Omar Khayyám's, or one of Emerson's essays. I could not only map out, in part, the trend of my fantasies, but could even lend color to the ecstatic stage of the keef trance. I saw to it, also, that my material environment was such as to suggest and sustain a lofty train of thought.[22] The appointments of my keef chamber, while they partook of Oriental luxury, were marked by the intellectual and refined taste of the Saracenic era and had nothing in common with the grosser forms and fleshly coloring of the Turkish School.

While under the spell of keef, I spent many hours in painting, and I could not but be pleased at the improvement shown by my work. Among my productions, at this period, were a "Tangierine Jewess"[23] and a study of "Dawn in the Desert." Chalmers, whose friendship and sympathy never failed me, was particularly enthusi-

"Tangierine Jewess."

"Dawn in the Desert"

astic over these pieces; and he was fond of insisting that for beauty of coloring and artistic truth they were distinctly superior to any of the canvases of Benjamin Constant.[24] But, in my passionate yearning after higher things, I remained unsatisfied and refused to exhibit my works. Much less would I put them on the market. Nothing short of the attainments of a Raffaele or an Angelo would content me.[25] Hopefully I labored on, putting my faith in keef and smoking unremittingly. While at work, with my brain steeped in the fumes of the wonder-working weed,[26] I was forever vexed by the intervention of unconsciousness. The coma which terminated my ecstasies was sure to come upon me all too soon, sealing my vision to the revelation that I sought, and barring the way to the inmost sanctuary of the Ideal which had become my God. The fault was in me, I argued, not in the drug. The grossness of my mind was such that the subtler intuitions, the lofty flights of soul, were beyond me. At times I caught myself wondering whether the missing element in my mental make-up was the experience of love, but this idea I put aside as frivolous. None the less, did I cling to the conviction that, by training and developing my better nature, I might compass the fulfilment of my desires. The sublime thoughts, which gem the masterpieces of literature, shone into my consciousness and seemed to impart to me something of the luminous inspiration of the authors. Accordingly, I burrowed in the books of the immortals and kept spiritual company with the greatest of the thinkers of earth. In this way months glided by. I seemed no nearer the coveted goal; but I was a child of golden hope, and somehow I felt sure that the word was yet to be spoken which should open for me the portal at which I sat and waited.

My one social relaxation, save for a rare and brief sojourn at the Siesta Club, was the companionship of Chalmers. He visited me well nigh daily. He brought me the newest books and the latest intelligence of the world from which I lived apart. There came an evening when he called upon me, and when, as was our custom, we sat and talked late into the night. That is, Chalmers talked and I listened in sympathy while he discoursed, in his inimitable and suggestive way, on literature, art and his favorite theme, the occult marvels of this mysterious universe. To me that night was

the Hegira to the Islamite.[27]   It stands in the same relation to my spiritual being which the day of my birth bears to my cruder self. When Chalmers had gone, I betook myself to my keef-pipe. While smoking, I picked up a volume which my friend had left, and of which he had spoken appreciative words. I was somewhat curious to learn the charm that the book held for him.[28] "A New Pygmalion" was a novel,[29] and Chalmers was accustomed to laud but few novels.   Again, it was a recent publication, anonymous, and, as my friend had informed me, the sensation of the day. Ordinarily, this, of itself, would have prejudiced my fastidious friend against the work. I opened the volume and scanned the pages listlessly, almost dreamily; but I had not proceeded far when the work stirred my interest. As I read, I found myself enthralled alike by the story and the style, and soon the recurring bother of replenishing my pipe became such a vexation that I rang for Hassan and imposed the task on him.

It was a simple tale. The hero was an author who, in his first romance, embodied in the heroine his ideal of womanhood. A copy of his book fell into the hands of a maiden on whom the portrayal of this heroine made so deep an impression that, unconsciously, she modeled her life and formed her character after the prototype who lived only on the printed page. In his maturity, the author, by a happy chance, met this maiden and, attracted by the very incarnation of his cherished fancy, wooed her and won her hand. Such was the story, but it was written with unique power. The writer of "A New Pygmalion" had a rare gift of impressing the reader with her own individuality. She had translated herself into her book. I say "she," and advisedly, for I had not finished the tale before I was convinced that the anonymous writer was a woman. There were passages in the story which spoke to me with the directness and personality of a lyric. A certain, dainty strength, a peculiarly tender, yet vigorous conception of life marked the work. The love scenes were palpitant with the pulsings of a woman's heart. There was in them a delicacy of tone, a sympathetic ideality of treatment, quite out of keeping with the masculine method in art. But the sovereign excellence and chief beauty of this matchless tale lay in the character of the heroine. Chalmers had lightly alluded to a

Liber Amoris; or, The New Pygmalion

William Hazlitt

DODO PRESS

"A New Pygmalion"

likeness which he fancied to exist between the hero and myself. The parity, if there was one, escaped me. Enough that we were alike in the one, paramount fact that we were both devoted to the heroine. The passion, which the women of my social world had failed to stir, was instantly fanned to a white heat by the breath of the unknown writer's genius. I was in love, madly in love, with the heroine of her creation. And, as I read and re-read, the conviction grew on me that the object of this sudden and supreme desire, the woman on whom, in that moment, I had centered all the interests of my soul, was no mere figment of imagination, but an existent being, purer, nobler, better than our kind, yet human as myself. In portraying a woman incomparably lovely in mind and person, I felt that the nameless writer had but projected her sweet self onto her page. While I abandoned myself to the spell of the novelist, I was conscious of a personality behind the book, tender, sympathetic, yet commanding withal. The style, chaste and strong, combined with the majesty of the great thoughts it clothes to lift me to a pitch of spiritual enthusiasm such as I had vainly striven after in my patient past. Could it be that this unknown writer had given voice to the message for which I waited, the words that I had sought in vain through the pages penned by the great ones of earth? From this little wayside spring, was I to dip the draught which should prove to me as the waters of life?

Even so—for, with the thought, I felt myself transfigured. The personality, which I had recognized as subtly pervading the volume in my hand, of a sudden, took to itself definite form and being. I was conscious of a presence close at hand, vague, at first, as the fumes of the keef that stained the candlelight, yet no less real. The next moment, I saw before me a vision of beauty so rare that the wonder is my spirit was not blasted by the contemplation of its loveliness. Standing by my side, as though risen from the storied page, I beheld the gracious shape of a woman whom I knew, at sight, for the ideal I had so long sought to conjure out of the chaos of my dreams.

Words cannot paint the ecstasy I now experienced. My soul was shaken with joy, as with mighty music. It seemed that my very body was quickened with angelic attributes, like the glorified body

"I saw before me a vision of beauty"

HASSAN AT WORK.

"Hassan, a Soudanese Negro of fabulous ugliness and gigantic stature"

of the Christian resurrection. I moved in a universe that was virgin to my thought, a world where matter and materialities were not, a realm of light and gladness and glamour which is not akin to earth and to describe which the language fashioned for the necessities of the lower life is all inadequate. If, in the opium trance, I was as Vathek in the Halls of Eblis,[30] now, surely, keef had taught me the joys of Adam in Paradise. In a spiritual Eden I wandered hand in hand with the fairest of womankind. I drank the love-light in her wistful eyes. I meshed my soul in the netted gold of her hair.

Bismillah! Blessed be keef.

The Spirit of "Haschisch" by S.H. Sime

"In a spiritual Eden... the fairest of womankind"

PHASE IV.

PHANTASM AND FLESH.

JUST how the keef trance merged into waking consciousness I cannot say. Certain it is that there must have intervened a period of unremembered activity, for I was startled to find a new canvas on the easel, and, on that canvas, sketched roughly in with a touch which I recognized as my own, the outlines of a new painting. Imagine my delight on finding that I had unwittingly obtained a sitting from the fair lady of my vision. I was jubilant at the prospect. Here was the promise that my loved one would brighten even my waking moments with her beauty. While the recollection of her charms was vivid enough to enable me to proceed with the work, I preferred to trust to the inspiration of the wonder-working drug, and I lost no time in renewing its influence.

I applied myself to my pipe, and again that perfect face and frame took unto themselves their subtle substance. My spirit bride approached and laid her hand upon my brow, as though sealing it with the signet of the genius that beamed from her majestic eyes. Again I experienced that ardent communion of souls which poets have inadequately sung, and which the mass of mortals have faintly imaged forth as the bliss unattainable of perfect love. Again there came the blank of unconsciousness, and again, on waking, I was overjoyed to find that notable progress had been made on the new painting. Thus matters went on for several weeks until the picture had grown, under my unconscious brush, into a flawless and completed work. Then it was that I could have fallen down and worshipped my own handicraft. Surely such a vision of human loveliness, whether in the flesh or on canvas, was never before vouchsafed to man.

The picture—or shall I not rather call it portrait—was scrupulously faithful, in coloring and outline, to the incomparable original; and faithful, too, not in the formal, photographic way but with that higher fidelity which seizes upon and reproduces character and life. There, definitely fixed, palpably present on the canvas,

A MARTYR TO HIS PASSIONS.

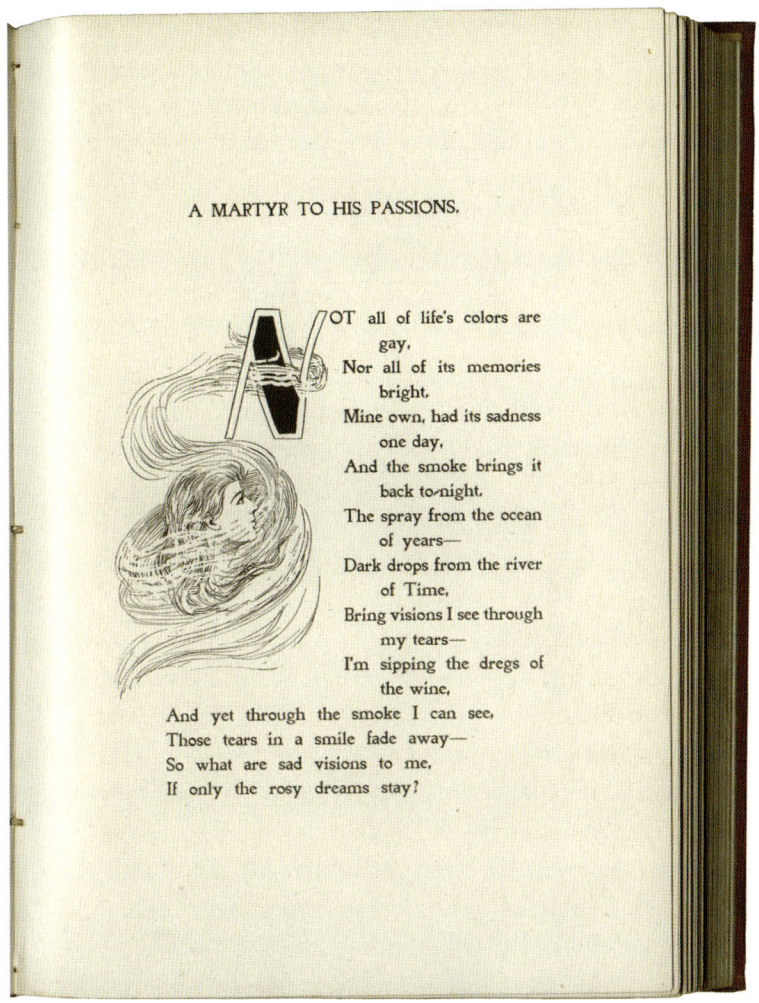

NOT all of life's colors are
gay,
Nor all of its memories
bright,
Mine own, had its sadness
one day,
And the smoke brings it
back to-night.
The spray from the ocean
of years—
Dark drops from the river
of Time,
Bring visions I see through
my tears—
I'm sipping the dregs of
the wine,
And yet through the smoke I can see,
Those tears in a smile fade away—
So what are sad visions to me,
If only the rosy dreams stay?

"risen from the storied page.... my spirit bride approached"

was the slender, queenly grace of my angel love. The exquisitely moulded head was wreathed with silken hair that took its hue from the sun's own rays, and now glistened yellow as gold in the high light, now glowed in the shadow with somber glories of bronze. Her eyes, luminous and inspiring as when in phantom worlds they flashed their message of love to me, were counterfeited on my canvas. Blue were they, a dark blue, deep and rich, and, through the shadowy growth of their luxuriant lashes, they shone with a mystic, gem-like fire.[31] Their splendor was vibrant now with passionate expectancy, and the lips, red-ripe and firm, yet delicate were faintly parted in aspiration. So looked she when she gave me greeting to the kingdom of the spirit.

To me this picture was at once a memento and a pledge. When my health threatened to break down utterly under the stress of too frequent indulgence in keef, I sought and found comfort in the contemplation of the canvas, while restoring my wasted frame. Then, too, there were times when, after several days of rigorous abstention from the drug, I became moody and skeptical, when I caught myself doubting the reality of my dual life and wondering whether I was the victim of a hallucination. The sense of loss and disenchantment which overwhelmed me on these occasions might have driven me mad, but for the possession of my previous canvas. I had but to step into my keef chamber and draw the silken hangings from the niche where I had mounted the painting, as a devotee might enshrine a Madonna, and I had before me the tangible and indisputable evidence of the truth of the higher existence and the love that sweetened it. Miracle or mystery it might be, if you will, but mistake—never. The most materialistic of men could not but admit that the picture, in conception and artistic treatment alike, was inspired in a nobler sense than any canvas given to the world by the masters of old. Sanzio the Divine himself,[32] never in his happiest touches approached the perfect beauty of my spirit bride.

That the phantasm I had prisoned on my canvas was that of the author of "A New Pygmalion," I did not doubt. The spirit which pervaded the book was one with the pure nature of the creature of my vision. It was clear that in the heroine Esther, the author had

"silken hair... glistened yellow as gold"

"Her eyes.... a dark blue, deep and rich"

sketched herself; and between the character of Esther and that of my spirit consort there was the matchless fitness of things, which constitutes ideal truth. In the course of time, I learned to call my dear one by that bright name with which she had christened the creature of her thought.

Through a natural desire to acquaint myself with the particulars of the earthly existence of my spirit bride, I made diligent inquiry in every practical quarter with a view to discovering the where-abouts and the conventional identity of the author—but without avail. The literary circles of the city were agog with a like curiosity, alike unsatisfied. I made use of my friend, Chalmers, to cultivate an acquaintance with all the women of the bookish set of the me-tropolis, hoping that I might come upon the object of my search; but the prim and lettered ladies whom I met were hopelessly un-like Esther. I longed to penetrate this mystery. Entrancing as were my daily trysts with Esther, in our exalted soul-communion, earth and the things of earth had no part. Our converse was as the pure mingling of spirit with spirit; and, after the sweet ecstasies of my keef visions, I returned to the material world as ignorant of her place therein as she doubtless was of mine. How could I be certain, even, that she had not been cut down by death, or that she might not be, to-day or to-morrow?

The weird communication, which I had entered into with the spirit world, in lieu of lessening my fear of death, increased it. I feared nothing so much as change. How could I know but that death might work some cunning change in my nature or hers that would forever bar me from her world? Annihilation would be preferable to the interruption of our intercourse. She had become merged in my inmost being. The words of "A New Pygmalion" I knew by heart and treasured as hers. Her face and form were as real and familiar to me as my own. I found myself looking at every woman with a new interest, for who could tell but that, at any mo-ment, I might stumble upon my Esther in the flesh?

My visits to the Siesta Club had grown infrequent and per-functory. I could not but contrast the atmosphere of the place with that of the flawless world through which my fair mate led me to the altars of the beautiful and the true. Of late, too, a certain

member of the club had caused me no little annoyance. This man, whose name was Ralph Black, was something of a connoisseur in paintings, having once dealt in them, in fact, and having cultivated that versatile aptitude for gauging values which is characteristic of the Shylock. He professed to be much taken with a portrait of Chalmers that I had painted some months before and presented to my friend. He looked down on me—he was a big man, ponderous and blonde and bland—and informed me that I "would do" and that I "could paint things that would sell." He was lavish of this unsentimental appreciation, made a point of being pleasant, in his unctuous, elephantine way, and inflicted his company upon me whenever he found me at the club. I was not long left in the dark as to his object. One night, he suavely proposed that I should paint his wife.

"You see," he said, "she's an invalid, and it'll be necessary to have the sittings at our home. There need not be any question about the price."

I curtly informed Mr. Black that I was not in the business of portrait painting, and declined out of hand to accede to his request.

Instinctively I hated this fellow. He was a Wall Street railroad-wrecker whose wealth was set at fabulous figures. There were queer stories about his methods. I had heard Chalmers say that Black belonged to many clubs, which he joined, as he had joined ours, from no spirit of comradery, but for the business purpose of studying, in its unguarded hours of social ease, the world on which he preyed. But then, he gave sumptuous dinners, and, with the beaus and bloods about town, it is a maxim that champagne drowns a multitude of sins. My refusal did not daunt him. He continued to thrust his attentions upon me, and concluded by inviting me to take dinner with him at his home. I guessed that by the blandishments of the entertainer he hoped to obtain as a favor what he could not buy as a service. Yet I accepted his invitation, mentally dooming him to disappointment, the while. Paint his wife I would not; but I could waive my objection to eating his dinner, and the opportunity to inspect the art treasures of which his house was said to be the repository was a temptation against which I was not proof.

When the appointed evening came, I found Mr. Black housed like a prince. From the hall, I was ushered by a sleek and stolid butler into a spacious reception room. On every hand, I was confronted with the evidences of refinement and taste. I had anticipated luxury, but to find a man of his type surrounded by an aesthetic atmosphere was something of a surprise. I accounted for this phenomenon by attributing it to the influence of the mistress of the household, and there were present in the decorations of the room in which I found myself, as well as of the parlors leading therefrom, certain, deft touches which predicated the presence of woman as positively as the prattlings of a nursery. There was an indescribable something in the grouping of furniture, a harmony in the hues and forms, that made of each room a poem with individual character. The soul of art was abroad in the house and sanctified it. The predominating sentiment was a delicate blending of the sensuous with the spiritual. Here a swinging censer, itself a priceless art fabric, anointed the air with the faint perfume of Persian roses. Yonder a glorious Magdalen in oil saluted heaven with moist eyes. A St. Cecilia, creditably done, hung near by. The gray melancholy of a Millet landscape had for its foil and offset a vivid sunset of Corot.

I found that my environment sensibly affected me. In the few moments that intervened before my host made his appearance, I was strangely impressed by the prevailing tone of the place, and I was seized with a sudden eagerness to meet the woman who had left the stamp of her personality on the material forms about me. When Black joined me, the contrast between him and his surroundings was so harshly emphasized as to be fairly painful. At the club he was simply obnoxious. To meet him here was to find a Goth in the gardens of Sallust,[33] to see the unbreached dominant in Versailles—in a word, to meet a moneychanger in the temple. Something of this he must have read in my face, but it did not disturb his serene complacency. He had the matter-of-fact self-possession of an animal.

He expressed his pleasure at seeing me. He was delighted, to be sure. Mrs. Black, too, would be pleased. An artist like myself would appreciate Mrs. Black. She was considered a mighty hand-

"The soul of art was abroad in the house and sanctified it."

"Magdalen... with moist eyes"

"gray melancholy of a Millet landscape"

"a vivid sunset of Corot"

some woman, and, if she were well enough to go into society, he guessed she'd throw some of the belles into the shade.

So he rattled on, while I listened in impassive contempt. His words grated on me. It was not their coarseness simply. I took a strange, pitying interest in this wife, delicately nurtured and high-minded, as I felt she must be, and I longed to take by the throat the clod who would seek to make a raree-show of her charms.

On the stillness, at this moment, there broke the echo of a step in the hall—faint, at first, from distance; then distinct; now muffled in the rugs that littered the tessellated floor; now clear and sharp in the open—a woman's step, light, elastic, firm; not, apparently, the tread of an invalid.[34] The next instant, the folds of a silken portiere were drawn aside, and my hostess entered.

I heard Black mumble some formula of introduction. I raised my eyes, and a chill like the rigor of death seized upon my every limb. My Esther stood before me in the flesh, queenly and radiant and beautiful with the more than mortal beauty that had dazzled me in my keef dream. The light of recognition in her glorious eyes was clouded by a passing shadow of perplexity, if not of pain. The commonplaces of greeting were frozen on her lips. Her gaze wandered slowly from my face to that of the man by my side. A sudden tremor came upon her, and the next moment she fell swooning in my arms.

I bore her across the room and laid her, limp and motionless, upon a sofa. This I did mechanically, for there had come to me that saving stupor which fences the mind against madness in the crucial moments of great emotion. All the while, I was conscious of contending against an imperative impulse to fold my dear one to my heart and kiss again the lips whose wine I had so often quaffed in our keef trysts.[35] But the chill, gray eye of the ogre Black pursued me and, alas![36] I knew that my bride in the mystic realm of spirit was his wife in the world of flesh.

He had never lost his imperturbable self-control for a moment. He assured me, as he rang for a maidservant, that there was no occasion for alarms, that his wife was subject to these attacks, and he begged me to be at my ease. I do not recall the terms of my reply.

"laid her, limp and motionless upon a sofa"

THE MEETING IN THE FLESH.

Portrait of Madame Hélène Vincent by Benjamin Constant, 1893

"queenly radiant.... the light... in her glorious eyes was clouded"

It was to the effect that I could not think of intruding at such a time. I took my leave at once and with scant ceremony. I was glad to gain the outer air. My heart was sick, my brain dizzy, and the pulses in my wrists and temples throbbed almost audibly.

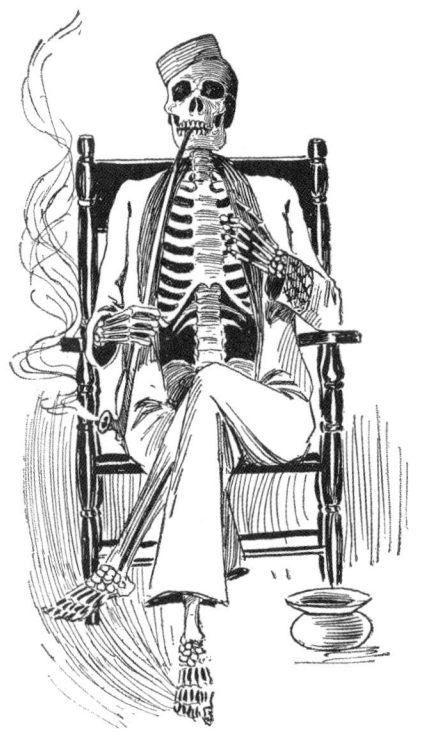

"My heart was sick... brain dizzy... pulses....throbbed"

PHASE V.

THE PASSING OF ESTHER.

FOR some days after this strange adventure, I was sorely harassed in mind. The stern discrepancy between my relations with Esther in our ideal life and those which fate had imposed upon us in the material world was, to me, a source of poignant anguish. Mingled with the pangs of personal loss, there was a keen regret that the irony of events should have condemned that pure and noble woman to the control of such a wretch as Ralph Black. That he was abhorrent to her I could not doubt. The faun does not consort with the satyr, the angel with the animal. The marriage of this brilliant, sensitive and high-minded woman to such a sordid, mercantile monster as Black could have had its origin in nothing short of compulsion. But married to him she was; and I knew that, however repugnant to natural law, the compact was hedged about with all the dignity of statutes and maintained by all the force of human conventions.

I nursed my grievance against fate and, while the wound in my heart was still green, I made successively many rash resolves. I vowed that I would raze the artificial barriers which civilization with its stupid laws had set between my love and me. I would tear my bride from this palace where a tyrant had immured her and bear her away to some secluded Eden-land in the distant, dreamful East. Failing in this, at least I could slay the man who stood between us. Or—and this, the latest suggestion lingered with me long—might not suicide for her and me be the best solution of the enigma?[37]

Such were the meditations to which my misery drove me; and I doubtlessly should have developed and put into execution one of these desperate plans were it not for a potent influence which was steadily at work, soothing and solacing me with a real and present joy. This was keef, my familiar. The fragrant vapors of my keef-pipe annulled the wretched accidents of the lower life, and transported me to the substantial beatitudes of the kingdom of the spirit. There Esther was still mine, and mine alone, giving herself

"vapors of my keef-pipe... transported me to.... Esther"

to me with the unrestraint of passion, and revealing to me, in the tender reciprocity of love, the infinite possibilities of a woman's devotion. Why, then, need I repine? After all, no social convention, no man-made code, no mummery of priest or magistrate could sever me from my spirit bride. The nominal union between her and Black, I argued, was not such as properly to cause me distress. It was essentially impossible that it could be a more intimate communion than that of the jailer and his victim. He might exert constraint over her person and her movements, but mental dominion, spiritual sympathy—these were my prerogatives. She had swooned in my presence, she came at my bidding, she illuminated my life with her love. I smoked and was content.

Still, I could not refrain from setting on foot certain inquiries touching the previous history of my beloved. I confided to Chalmers enough of my strange experience to interest him in the quest, and, through his investigations, I was soon in possession of the outlines of Esther's sad story. To be sure, the details that he gathered were made up mostly of the hints which club men whisper over their wine, but, when strung together, they formed a narrative sufficiently succinct and bearing intrinsic evidences of truth.

Esther was the only child of a diamond merchant whose wealth, culture and magnificence had, for years, lent a splendor to the fashionable society of the city. Her mother had died while she was yet a girl. Dowered with a bewildering physical beauty, and with rare brilliancy of mind, she found herself, upon her Coming Out, the petted darling of society, beleaguered by admirers on all sides.[38] She accepted homage and rejected suitors; both as a matter of course. At twenty-two years of age, she wrote and published "A New Pygmalion." Its success was such that she might well have been ready to avow it as the product of her pen, and she undoubtedly would have broken the seal of secrecy but for a calamity that befell her father and which had for her a fateful sequence. The exact character of this mischance was not known. It had to do with certain operations in Mexican mining stock. It involved financial failure, certainly, and, possibly, social disgrace. These consequences were averted by the timely intervention of the broker, Ralph Black. There were not wanting those who said that Black had enticed the

old merchant into a trap, with a view to rescuing him at the eleventh hour for a good and sufficient consideration, and that Esther was that consideration. The rumor of the merchant's impending insolvency was met simultaneously by a denial and by the unexpected announcement of his daughter's marriage to Black. The ceremony was secret, and, from the day of its celebration, the brilliant, society belle had lived the life of a recluse. She had now been married six months, and, during that period, she had never graced a social function. The mask of the author of "A New Pygmalion" was never formerly lifted. This, said the knowing ones, was not to be wondered at, since one of the characters in the story, the villain of the tale, was a realistic and thinly veiled portrait of Ralph Black. Awesome mockery of fate that gave the fair, young author to the keeping of a husband whom she loathed and whom she had pilloried by her art. One week after her marriage, Esther's father died. Had he thought of doing so a few days earlier, he would have rendered needless a voluntary sacrifice that had in it the direful elements of a blood atonement.

Such was the gloomy narrative that I contrived to piece together—a melancholy mosaic of my own inferences and the bits of information gathered by Chalmers. When I had digested the story, I felt more strongly than ever that Esther was indeed mine, and that she had not and never could have had anything in common with the creature who called himself her husband. Yet, despite the ravishments of our keef trysts, I could not but feel interested in her physical environment and welfare.[39] In the intervals of my keef visions, I took to patrolling the streets about her house by night, watching, with a lover's fond infatuation, the play of lights in the windows, and wondering which of the countless rooms in the great mansion held the treasure that occupied my thoughts. After a time, I plucked this precious secret from a servant whom I corrupted with tips. Then I had won a new happiness. I spent hours at a time in the shadows of the corner opposite the dwelling, straining my eyes at the lace that draped her windows. Only to be near her was a delight,[40] giving me, as it did, a vague sense of guardianship. To catch a glimpse of her figure silhouetted against the window shade was to be transported with joy. How my heart

went out during those solitary vigils in fervent wishes for her well-being! The aspirations I breathed there in the dark had in them something akin to the ardor and unselfishness of perfect prayer. Now and again I detected myself in the act of uttering an impassioned apostrophe; and it is certain that, more than once, I flung kisses at my loved one's curtained windows with all the extravagance of an amorous boy.

It was after a vigil of this sort that, as I was returning home one wintry night, I suddenly became aware that I was followed. The tall figure of a man, swathed in a voluminous topcoat, was dogging my footsteps with the pertinacity of a shadow. The man kept at some distance behind me and regulated his gait by mine. When I halted, he turned into a side street, only to re-appear in my wake when I proceeded on my way. Gauging his pace, I calculated the moment when he would necessarily walk under the searching rays of an arc light that I had just passed. When that moment arrived, I pivoted about suddenly and scanned my pursuer. He was not fifty yards away and I recognized him at once. Strangely agitated, I resumed my walk and, on reaching my abode, entered it without looking back. The man who had shadowed me was Ralph Black; and I had seen that his face, livid under the eerie glamour of the electric light, was convulsed and distorted by passion into the semblance of a tragic mask.

It was apparent that he was suspicious of me—jealous, perhaps. Somehow his attention had been called to my nightly vigils.[41] Possibly, he had connected these with the agitation which I had betrayed on the occasion of my memorable meeting with his wife. In any case, it was plain that, to save Esther embarrassment, I must discontinue my visits to the neighborhood of his house. I managed, however, to maintain my watch over my beloved in another way. Through the domestic whom I still contrived to keep in my pay, I received full and frequent reports of the goings-on in the Madison Avenue mansion.[42]

From this source, I learned that there was a permanent estrangement between husband and wife, barely glozed over in the immediate presence of the servants by the most conventional of courtesies. I learned, too, that the mysterious malady which afflicted the

John Jacob Astor

"a tall figure... in a voluminous topcoat"

"countless rooms.... goings-on in the Madison Avenue mansion"

mistress of the household showed no signs of abating; that, at the most unexpected moments, the lady would fall in a faint and gradually pass into a trance-like state in which she would lie for hours. These attacks were increasing in severity, and, for some time back, had been of daily occurrence. The affliction, so far, had proved absolutely beyond the control of the doctors. The best experts on nervous diseases in the city had been in attendance and had agreed in their diagnoses. It was, said they, a pronounced case of hysteria, unaccompanied by functional disturbance and without any of the symptoms of organic disease.[43] They agreed, too, that, if the attacks continued, death by exhaustion must shortly supervene. One of the peculiar features of the case was that the fair patient seemed in no wise distressed by her critical condition, had none of the dread of an attack which characterizes the ordinary cataleptic, and contemplated the prospect of speedy death with the greatest cheerfulness.

This information I obtained piecemeal and from time to time, so that it did not immediately occur to me that this novel ailment, which baffled the physicians, was referable to the ascendancy that I had gained over the mental life of Esther. No sooner, however, did I appreciate this likelihood, that I set out to confirm or disprove the theory by conclusive experiments. For several weeks I made a point of chronicling the hour and the moment at which I sought the solace of my keef-pipe. On comparing this record with the information subsequently brought to me, I found that my keef visions and the swooning fits, which perplexed the doctors, were uniformly simultaneous and co-extensive in duration. I further learned that these peculiar attacks had begun at the very period when, under the magic spell of keef, I read, for the first time, "A New Pygmalion."[44] I desisted from smoking for several days. During this period, the afflicted lady was exempt from the fainting fits. I reverted to the drug, and the strange malady asserted itself at once.

I now found myself face to face with a problem the solution of which was fraught with the weightiest consequences both to my beloved and myself. It was clear that to continue to induce my keef visions was, by implication, to pass sentence of death on Esther. Was I justified in taking such a course? For the consequences

to myself I did not care. I had now been addicted to the almost daily use of keef for eight months, and my physical system was fast sinking under the stress of abnormal stimulation. The constant inhalation of the powerful vapors of the drug had affected my lungs. I had a cough, night-sweats and other pulmonary weakness. My nervous energies were impaired, and the spectre, insomnia, was my frequent bedfellow. I had sought no physician. I was familiar, through study, with the physiological effects of keef, and knew that to persist in the consumption of the drug meant death, and death preceded, mayhap, by mania. But I had stared the future in the face without ceasing to smoke for a day. Death had no terrors for me now. Experience had convinced me that the higher flights of soul were retarded, rather than assisted, by the activity of the bodily functions, and I knew that to be released from the bondage of the flesh was to be franked forever as a citizen of that bright universe wherein it had been given me to meet my spirit bride. Surely every selfish interest should prompt me to continue my indulgence in the drug and thus speed the day which would bring me nearer to my dear one.

But Esther's welfare, and that alone, was my controlling thought. I hesitated to impose on her the ordeal of dissolution that I welcomed for myself. In my perplexity, I abandoned keef for the space of a week or more. The tortures, which I had suffered during previous periods of abstention, seemed tripled now, tortures of mind and body, agony of soul, caused by the self-imposed isolation from my bride, and the racking physical pangs of the outraged nerves that craved their wonted stimulant.[45] It was after learning that, throughout this interval, Esther, while improved in physical health, was the prey of an abiding melancholy that my final resolution was taken. It was plain that the severance of our intercourse meant suffering for her no less than for myself. Better by far that she should die the death of the flesh than that she should linger on in the lower life, saddened in spirit, and linked to an alien destiny. Death for her would be emancipation. The doubts, which had assailed me, now gave way to a sense of perfect peace. I invoked again the sorcery of keef and joyfully anticipated the issue.

At rare intervals I went with Chalmers to the club. Black was seldom there. On the few occasions when I met him, there was a marked embarrassment in his manner. At times, I fancied that I could detect in his eyes something of the sombre and vengeful glow, which I had remarked on the night when he dogged me in the streets. It did not surprise me to hear that he had tried to coax from Chalmers certain particulars as to my character and antecedents.

Three months after my return to the use of keef, Esther died. She passed away in a trance. Hers was an idyllic death. She simply forgot the strife, the suffering and the sinning of the world; and the memory of misery never came back to her. Her passing was but the sequel to a love tryst. She fell asleep in my bosom, and never knew again the pain of waking to the unrealities of earth.

Unbidden, I went to the house of death. In the hush of the taper-lit parlor, I looked unmoved on the marble beauty of the body that had been hers. Unbidden, I followed the funeral train to the grave and stood by at the burial, with undimmed eyes. I had not cause to mourn. The insensate clay, which they gave back to earth, was not my bride. The coffin held the wife of Ralph Black. It was not Esther. That radiant and immortal spirit had passed from the purgatory of the flesh into a heaven of light and love. She was mine for time and for eternity. I knew that in that very moment she waited for me on the threshold of the home of ideal love.

"I followed the funeral train to the grave"

THE UNBIDDEN MOURNER.

From the time her husband Ali died "Zuleyka clothed herself in thick veils and re-
nounced the pleasures of the world. She withdrew into the solitude of a quiet house,
she mourned Ali and lived in memory of him.
But she did not remain idle. She, the childless one, had many children: the poor, the
sick and the helpless were her children."

– from Haschisch by Fritz Lemmermayer

Editor's Note
Zuleyka confessed all of her sins and absolved Ali from his in the name of love.
He died of an overdose, smoking haschisch from a hookah shaped from a skull
[see page 166].

PHASE VI.

ASHES TO ASHES.

How shall I describe the splendor that entered into my keef ecstasies with the passing of Esther from the prison-house of the flesh! The raptures of my earlier visions were multiplied, and the joy of dwelling in the ideal world wherein my Esther now had her abiding-place was rarer, keener than before. There had been times when the magic of my precious drug was slow to work, and the coming of Esther to the keef tryst, delayed. This was occasioned, most likely, by the unfavorable conditions of her environment and the adverse influences of Black's personality. Now she was free, and to be free was to be mine. She lingered ever at the frontier of the senses and beckoned me to bliss. Small wonder, then, that I abandoned myself to the witching drug, which proffered me hourly the open-sesame to the kingdom of life. Night and day, I kept the incense of keef burning on the altar of my love. For me, the external universe, that chaos of shadows in conflict which men call the world, ceased to have significance. I never went abroad. I lost all track of dates and days. Needless to say, I did not paint. From the hour when I put the last touches to the sublime canvas on which I had materialized the face and form of Esther, I never took brush in hand. And this, I reasoned, was just and seemly. In painting Esther I had attained the acme of art; I had grasped ideal perfection. For him who has dwelt in the seventh heaven there is no promise of joy in the allurements of a lower paradise.

It was late autumn when Esther entered into peace, and one night, soon after the funeral, the winter swooped down upon the city. A sudden blizzard gagged the streets with snow and stifled the rioting voices of the town. Only the measured rumblings of the elevated trains survived the assault of the storm. These boomed, now and again, through the curtained depths of my keef chamber—echoes of the dread artillery on the battlefield of life. I lay on the divan, caressing the trusty keef-pipe which now seldom left my hand during my conscious hours. I was spent with bodily weakness, and at intervals I coughed desperately. A week before,

a physician whom Chalmers insisted on calling in had clapped a stethoscope to my wasted ribs, had listened learnedly through a brace of rubber tubes and finished by tabooing keef and prescribing Colorado.[46] I had smiled at him, and, after his departure, I discussed with Chalmers, in a philosophic spirit, what my friend chose to call my "suicide." I failed to win from him outright acquiescence in my course, yet I could not but feel that his reproaches sprang from the strength of personal affection rather than from any weakness of his reason, and that he knew in his heart that mine was the way of wisdom; for I had told him enough of my esoteric history to convince him that loss of life would mean for me an infinite gain in living.

On the tall easel in the alcove that fronted my couch, stood the material embodiment of my beloved Esther. The constant beauty of her face caught new and fickle graces from the flames that spurted in the great fireplace, quilting the candlelight with fantastic patterns. As I looked upon the marvel on the canvas, I recalled the dumb, delightful ecstasy of Chalmers when I had set before him, for one jealous moment, this last unanswerable argument in the cause of keef and love. From that instant, he had ceased to rebuke me for my devotion to the mystic drug. Poor fellow! I knew that I had bought his silence at the expense of his peace of mind. From that hour, I saw in his eyes the soul-hunger of one to whom the vision of bliss has been vouchsafed only to be withdrawn, and I pitied him for the hopeless desire, which the glimpse of Esther's perfections had kindled in his heart.

My reverie was molested by the stealthy, sandalled footfall of my giant nurse, black Hassan. He surprised me with a visiting card. My only callers were Chalmers and the doctor, and their visits were paid without the medium of any such formal announcement. To the big Soudanese, the bit of pasteboard was clearly a thing of fateful import, a hieroglyphic talisman that had aroused all the fetishism of his native desert. He held it gingerly and surrendered it with apparent relief.

The inscription on the card startled me into a momentary confirmation of the Negro's empty alarms. The name was the name of Ralph Black. I composed my face and ordered Hassan to show

in the visitor. Rising, meanwhile, not without physical pain, I hurriedly drew the silken screen over the picture of my beloved. The next moment, I was back on my couch, blowing wreaths of aromatic incense into space.

I greeted Black nonchalantly, almost flippantly.

"Pray be seated and make yourself at home!" I said.

The man ignored alike my invitation and the ill-disguised mockery of my tone. For a full minute he stood voiceless, staring at me with stolid face. His colossal shape dwarfed everything in sight. Surely, in the gross world of matter, this mammoth was king by right divine of superior bulk. As he towered before me, I recalled the malevolence pictured on those massive features, in the white glare of the electrics, the night he followed me home from my vigil under Esther's window. His countenance was haggard now, and had a strained, set look that was newer to me than the baleful, detective gleam in his eyes.

I had no conversational nothings to offer the man. His very presence in the place consecrated to art, to Esther and to love, savored, to my mind, of sacrilege. I resumed my pipe and waited in silence until he should disclose his errand, if errand he had. At last he spoke, briefly and to the point, with a cold formality in his voice, akin to that impassive fixity of face that the fire that lived and leaped in his eyes belied.

"Abecassis," he said, "I have come to renew an old request. You can do me the greatest kindness one man ever did another; and you are the only man in all the world who can do this thing. I want to ask you to paint the portrait of my wife."

"Your wife? Yours?" I interposed.

The sneer was scarce suppressed, but it was lost on Black. At least, he gave no sign of resentment.

"My wife—my dead wife," he went on. "You can do it from memory. You have the skill, the art, and you have seen her. Artists do not forget the faces of the beautiful—and she was beautiful. I know you have not forgotten her."

The man spoke this last slowly, tentatively, focusing his glowing eyes on me the while, as though they were torches to light him to the secret places of my soul. I looked him in the forehead, un-

flinchingly—more—defiantly.

"I have forgotten nothing—and forgiven nothing," I said.

Black turned on his heel, and, walking to the window, stood peering through the snow-flecked pane into the storm. His tense posture and twitching fingers spoke of the excitement that bade fair to master his iron nature. After a time, he came over to me, with the sudden and eager movement of the gambler who plays his last trump.

"They told me you were sick, Abecassis—dying," he said. "But you shall not die until you have done this thing for me. And not then, if it is your will to live. For, between us, we have gold enough to fight off even death. Listen, Abecassis, I angered you once by offering you money. I was wrong in that, but it was not till afterwards that I learned that you were rich. Don't misunderstand me now. I offer you now, not money, but wealth, my fortune, riches so vast that, united to your own, they will make of you a force among men greater than the power of parliaments, or congresses, or kings. Listen! You have learning and talents. Add to your means the millions which I can and will deliver, and you can make the world your carriage and mankind your footman. All that I ask, in return, is a few hours of effort that will cost you nothing, that will not make your mind the poorer by a thought, that will not steal so much as a touch from the cunning of your hand. For God's sake, don't say 'No!' Promise me you'll paint the picture—her picture. I beg you to promise. See! I'm begging."

His speech was headlong, breathless. He had thrown himself on his knees, and groveled there, pleading.

It may have been piteous, but it only seemed grotesque to me.

My brain tingled with the subtle intoxication of keef. A mocking devil danced in my heart. Strength came to me—a strength born of the spirit of scorn and reprisal. I leaped from the divan and ripped aside the drapery that hid the prisoned phantom of my bride.

"Look!" I cried. "Look! Do you recognize the likeness?"

Black rose and stood rooted and dumb, like a man enchanted, smitten by the spell of beauty. His gaze was riveted on the canvas. He seemed unconscious of my words—of everything, save only

the vivid presence on the easel.

At last he spoke, thickly, feverishly:

"From memory?"

"From life," I replied, "throbbing, clinging, odorous, amorous life. From hourly, daily, nightly sittings. Fool! The lady whom you call your dead wife was and is my living bride, my deathless mate."

I was beside myself. I know not all I said, but I did not lack for phrases. Words flew from me, winged and hissing, like arrows from a well bent bow; rancorous, stinging words, apt and fit to bite their way into a heart of bronze and poison all the springs of consciousness.

I pointed to a copy of "A New Pygmalion" that lay on the table at my side, and reminded Black that in the book the Sibylline genius of Esther had laid bare the spiritual deformities of his nature. I upbraided him for constraining that noble being to link her earthly fortunes with his sordid lot. He had profaned a jewel, and it had turned to cinder in his hand. He was free to reclaim the clay that he had given to the worms; but Esther, I boasted as mine, mine alone. I claimed her for my own before high heaven and to his teeth—mine for all time, for eternity, my love, my dearest one, my own.

Black heard me out, standing stiff and silent, as before. Could it be that his muddy blood remained unstirred by my gibes? Ah! No. The charm that bound him was the picture. I noticed now that his eyes were fixed unfalteringly on the painted shape of Esther. They had lost their sullen fire, and in them was a wondrous tenderness, together with something of the nameless entreaty which graces the gaze of the dumb. Nothing could have goaded me to the fury with which that look inspired me. Had this swine, then, so keen an appetite for husks? Good! He should feed his fill upon them. The picture should be his, but as Esther was his—in nothingness.

"Black," I said, "I need no painted image to keep my sweetheart's memory in my soul. This is but the shadow of a substance that is forever mine, and the shadow shall cease from this moment. You have locked away the dust of what you called your wife. Stay, and you may gather again the ashes of an immortal beauty."

The Oval Portrait by J.P. Laurens, 1895

"From life... throbbing, clinging... odorous, amorous life"

THE MIRACLE ON THE EASEL.

John Jacob Astor III

"stolid face... colossal shape... king by right divine of superior bulk"

Frenzy lent me strength to carry out the whim that had seized upon my fancy. In a trice, I tore the picture from its easel, dragged it from the alcove and hurled it far into the flaming cavern of the great fireplace.

For a second, Black seemed dazed by the unexpected movement. The next instant, with the single word "Madman!" he flung himself upon me and threw me back upon the divan. His thick and bony fingers choked the outcry in my throat. I was weak and wasted by illness, and my puny struggles availed nothing. I saw the big veins in his forehead swollen to a horrid purple. His eyes fairly stabbed at mine. They were strained and bloodshot and lurid with the menace of murder. I caught the flash of white metal. I hear the click of a revolver and against my hot and drumming temple I felt the cold muzzle of the weapon. Then my jaded nerves failed me and I lost consciousness.

PHASE VII.

THE ATAVISM OF HASSAN.

WHEN I came to myself, I found that I was the prisoner of a temporary paralysis, which held me as helpless on my couch as if I had been bound hand and foot. A few feet away, stretched full length on the marble floor, Ralph Black and my servant Hassan lay locked in each other's arms and wrestling to the death. Powerless to aid, and scarce awake to my own vital concern in the issue of the fight, I watched the wrestlers with a lazy, artistic interest, as if theirs were an alien combat, and I a chance spectator.

Physically, the men were well matched. Black had the advantage in weight; possibly, too, in sheer, brute strength. Hassan excelled him in agility, in height and reach. Both were powerful, well-groomed animals, in the very pink and prime of life, superb types of their respective races. Evidently, the hand-to-hand conflict had already lasted some time, for both men were glowing with heat and puffing with the exertion of the fight. Black was hampered by his snugly fitting garb of fashionable cut, while Hassan's Eastern costume gave loose and easy play to his every movement. They were on their feet now, and Black was making a frantic effort to lift his antagonist and hurl him to the floor. At one moment, Hassan's long, lithe back and turbaned head hung balanced and vacillating above the brawny trunk of his adversary; but directly the Negro regained his footing and, by a dexterous manoeuvre, tripped his opponent, bringing him to his knees. In half a minute, Hassan was dragged down by the white man, and the battle was resumed upon the floor.

To and fro, under and over, the giants tumbled, in a desperate contest for the mastery. Now Hassan won a brief supremacy and appeared poised upon the boulder-like frame of his adversary, only to be toppled over the next instant, when, by a mighty output of his Titanic strength, Black got the upper hand and, for the moment, held him down. During these checkered vicissitudes of the struggle, limb groped for limb, arm gripped arm, and knee clenched knee, as if by a sort of instinct; so that it seemed as though the very

Dag by Brady, N.Y.   Eng'd by Smillie.

joints and sinews of the gladiators were their conscious partners in the fight.

Clearly, the aim of each man was to pin his opponent to the floor and choke him into submission. Scarcely an arm's-length away, and between my couch and the heads of the wrestlers, there shone on the floor the pearl-handled pistol with which Black had attempted my life. It was plain that my faithful serving-man had flung himself on my assailant just in the nick of time, knocking the weapon from his hand; and I readily guessed that the duel I now witnessed was a fight for the possession of the pistol.

Of a sudden, Black's right arm unlaces itself from the Negro's hold, and his eager fingers snatch convulsively at the coveted weapon, but Hassan's left lunges out to checkmate the movement. Elbow hooks elbow again, and the deadlock remains unbroken. Still clinging to his adversary, the supple Hassan squirms, twists and slips from under, and the giants lie sidewise, parallel, and eye-to-eye, in a strenuous embrace of hate. The white man struggles with a rigid face, dogged and silent, after the manner of the Saxon who fights for his life. Hassan wastes his wind in eloquent, Arabic blasphemies that blow through his set teeth like the hiss of escaping steam.

Balked in his latest attempt, Black nerves himself for a super-human effort, and pushing the huge momentum of his big body at the resisting Hassan, using his massive knee as a lever, he again succeeds in getting the Soudanese under him. He grapples at the Negro's throat, only to be foiled by the clutching hand of the wary, black man. Whenever he manages to free an arm from the grape-vine grip of the Negro, Black rains blow after blow, with clenched fist, on the face, neck and body of his opponent. This style of war-fare is plainly unfamiliar to Hassan, and, when he seeks to reply in kind, his clumsy passes are warded from vital points by the arts of the boxer.

Both men are spent and panting painfully now. But there is no truce, as there is to be no quarter. With congested faces and distended eyes, they tear at each other like fiends. Black's straw-like hair reeks with sweat. It glistens in beads on his cheeks and forehead. It drips onto the steaming neck of the Negro. Suddenly,

with one gigantic tug, the white man wrenches the body of his opponent several inches from the floor and hurls it, with all the added weight of his own, great frame, back again upon the marble. Hassan's head crashes upon the stone, and, on the instant, his long, elastic arms fall limp and lifeless to the floor, the taut muscles of his black calves relax, his chin drops, and the pupils desert his eyes, leaving the upturned whites to stare blind and deathlike into the remorseless face of his opponent.

It is over now. I see the lumbering shape of Black lurch heavily forward, eclipsing the inert and sprawling form of his vanquished foe. His fingers close on the pistol-butt. A sense of the folly of an outcry in that great, silent house taunts me at the moment, and yet I essay to shout aloud. In vain. I am not only bedridden, but speechless.

In the next breath, I beheld a marvel of bodily prowess that seemed incredible. Hassan had risen from the dead. His face, buried under the overlying bulk of his opponent, I could not see, but I saw his long and sinewy arms flash out and close like talons about the great, bull neck of his adversary. I saw his legs—twin serpents, bare, black and quivering—spring aloft, vivid with the play of corded muscle, and twine themselves like a whiplash about Black's mighty limbs. I saw—nay, I felt—the tense and vibrant strain of Hassan's every sinew as, with a quick, nervous jerk, he pulled down the head of the white man till it rested, cheek by jowl, alongside its black fellow in a resistless and demoniac caress. The African was silent now. The white man lay motionless, an ox passive in the coils of a boa constrictor. The pistol had fallen from his inert fingers, and over his visage there crept a horror of agony that sickened me as I looked.

What had come upon the Anak[47] that had robbed him of his powers? His huge body lay idle as a corpse. Only the spasm in his face and the mute agony of his beseeching eyes bespoke him conscious still. His tongue protruded between his lips. A livid, purple flush came into his cheeks as I watched, and his breathing, which had seemed to cease, became audible and echoed in the silence, rasping and stertorous—a long-drawn groan, measured, monotonous, maddening to the ear. At that moment, he would have

served for a model of the condemned undergoing the penalty of the garrote, and I should have said unhesitatingly that Hassan had throttled him, were it not that the lean and claw-like hands of the black Hercules were plainly in my view, knitted and interlaced into a living lock at the back of the white man's burly neck.

In another second, the mystery of it all was made only too clear, for, trickling down from under the white man's head, oozing out into the spectral candlelight, across the mosaic of colored tiles, and staining them with a more vivid and fearsome hue, I saw a rivulet of blood—human blood—the blood of Hassan's victim, Ralph Black. It all flashed on me now. The black man's swoon was a sham, the ruse of a barbarous brain. Thrown off his guard, in his murderous haste to regain control of his revolver, the white giant had exposed to his foe that one spot which is, of all others, the most vulnerable in a duel between unarmed men—the throat. And in that critical moment, the domestic training of years and all the schooling of civilized associations were wiped out for Hassan. The wild atavism of his desert blood stirred in his fevered veins. He forgot even to be a Mussulman.[48]   He was only the tribesman of the Soudan, and he obeyed the brutish impulse to bury his teeth in the flesh of his enemy.

The horror of it gave me back my voice. With a supreme effort, I half-lifted myself from the divan and shouted at the Negro a frightful, Arabic curse.

"Up, you beast!" I cried. "Shall a son of the Prophet feed on the carrion of an infidel? Up, this instant! The white devil is dead."

Sullenly, reluctantly, but at the word, the loyal savage disentangled himself from the form of his opponent and rose to his feet. He stood before me cringing under the sting of my reproaches, like a mastiff after a whipping. But reason had returned to him, and he said pleadingly:

"Allah knows that he would have taken your life, my master."

I did not choose to look him in the face, for I knew that there was that upon it the thought of which was enough to make me shudder.

"Look you, Hassan," I replied. "Life is a small matter. But great is Mohammed, and great is the Koran of Mohammed. You have

GUERRIERS SOUDANAIS   S. I. P.

"he was only the tribesman of the Soudan"

broken the law of the Prophet. If you would make your peace with Allah, bind up the wound you have opened."

The habit of submission reasserted itself. The Negro made a low salaam, saying, simply: "*Bismillah,*[49] I obey."

And forthwith the honest fellow unwound the scarf of his turban, and kneeling by the prostrate form of his enemy, proceeded adroitly to bind and knot the improvised bandage about Black's bleeding throat. I noticed, however, that he first took the precaution to pick up the pistol which had been the bone of contention and thrust it into the folds of his sash.

It was a needless provision. For, while Black had never lost consciousness, and was even now greatly revived, the fever of strife had been drained out of him. He trembled from head to heel, and when, after several attempts to rise, he finally got his footing, he wavered unsteadily, like a candle-flame in a draught. He had lost his nerve. He spoke no word. Silently, with eyes averted, he staggered to the door, groping as he went, like a sleepwalker. We heard him stumble down the staircase, and the clangor of the outer door, slamming at his back, told us that he had gained the street.

The scene had so exhausted me that he had scarcely gone before I fell into a heavy, comatose sleep by which I was greatly composed and refreshed. When I woke, it was day. The storm had passed, and the morning was sparkling with sunlight and white with the jewels of the snow.

"the honest fellow unwound the scarf of his turban"

PHASE VIII.

A COMMONPLACE TRAGEDY.

THE melodramatic visit that Mr. Black had done me the honor to make was an episode very far from my liking. The long habit of mental ease to which I had accustomed myself, and my studied isolation from the jarring influences of the rude and unreal outer world, made the experience positively painful in retrospect. The excitement of the fact itself, the rush of incident and movement, had blinded me, for the moment, to the harmful effect on my spiritual temperament of this unwonted abandonment of self to the passions of the flesh. But wisdom came to me with the morning, and, in the peace of my keef-pipe brought to my vexed soul, I determined that I would put the sea between me and the possibility of a similar shock.

Besides, I now persuaded myself that Black had called upon me with the deliberate purpose of murder, and that his preliminary parley was a stratagem, designed to entrap me into such an admission as would fully justify him to himself for the act that he contemplated.

To what length might he not go in furtherance of his revenge? I did not dread a personal assault, and death had no terrors for me; but it occurred to me that Black might invoke the courts. On what ground, or by what process, I knew not; but he had left my house a wounded man, and grim forebodings of warrants, police justices, jails even, and all the monstrous machinery of the law, haunted me.

The prospect of any interruption of my intercourse with Esther, the possibility of the deprivation of keef, this was a danger, which appalled me to think of. I could not afford to take chances.

My resolution once taken, I put it into effect forthwith, as was my habit in such matters. A steamship of the French line was due to sail for Europe at the turn of the tide. I had six hours in which to perfect arrangements. It was ample time. Hassan fetched me a dealer who took my house and furnishings off my hands, after brief bargaining. My keepsakes and personal belongings were soon packed, and midday found me cozily quartered in a state-

"A steamship of the French line was due to sail for Europe"

room of *La Sylphide*[50] outward bound for Havre.[51]

My destination, of course, was Tangiers, the city of my birth, the home of all the dreams that peopled my vivid youth, the site of the House of Visions, the garden place where men sow keef and gather, in a finite world, the flowers of the infinite. The sublime inertia of the Orient stole upon me with the mere sense of journeying eastward.

We had passed Hellgate and were steaming down the Sound, when, in a listless moment, I picked up the morning papers—a dissipation I had not known for months. These headlines in *The Daily Interviewer* caught my eye at once:[52]

SUICIDE OF RALPH BLACK

Popular Millionaire Puts a Bullet in his Brain

Victim of Business Worry and Overwork

This was the story that followed:

Another victim of business cares and the prostration of overwork has been added to the list of suicides. This morning, a few minutes after midnight, the sharp report of a pistol startled belated pedestrians in the neighborhood of Ralph Black's palatial residence on Madison Avenue. A group of frightened servants rushed on to the stoop and called lustily for help. When the policeman on the beat made his appearance, he learned from the butler that the shot had been fired, apparently, in Mr. Black's private suite, the doors to which were securely locked from within. Mr. Black, the butler said, had come in late, as was his habit, and had gone directly to his rooms.

The policeman put himself at the head of an exploring party forthwith. On ascending to the millionaire it was found necessary to force the door of his chamber. Within, the electric light was found turned on, and the bed unfumbled. Passing to the marble bath, the party came upon a gruesome sight. Lying on his back, his head bathed in a pool of blood that flowed from a smoke-blackened hole above the right temple, was the master of the house. He was quite dead. The weapon of death, a five-barrelled revolver, with an empty shell in one chamber, lay by his side. A bloodstained scarf, with the initial "A" worked in the corner, swathed his neck.

Sylphide Schooner, Namesake of the Steamship

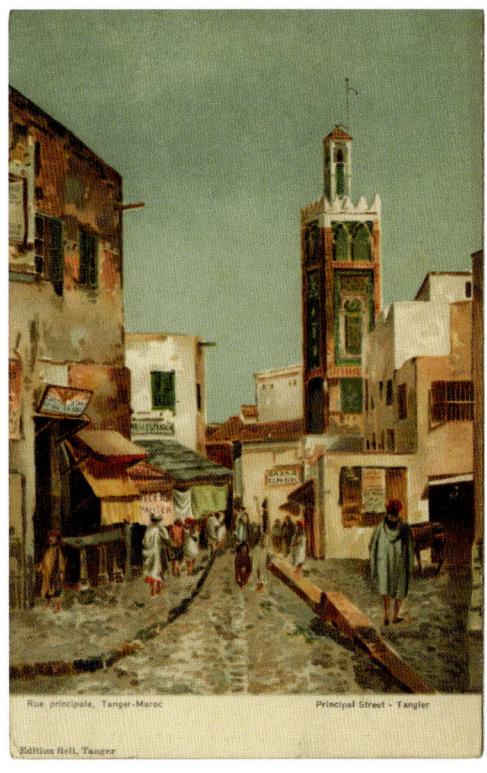

"the home of all the dreams that peopled my vivid youth"

It is the theory of the police that the deceased first attempted to cut his throat and, not meeting with a speedy result, seized upon the revolver as the agent of a ready and quicker death. This theory is borne out by the fact that an examination of the throat of the deceased revealed recent lacerations, evidently made by some sharp instrument.

As I tossed the paper aside and threw myself back into the embrace of my steamer-chair, my look lighted on the mahogany face of Hassan who sat squatted on his heels at my feet. His eyes snapped with the zest of being noticed, and, through the rift of his bearded lips, I saw his white teeth flash like bayonets in the sun.

The *Morning Universe*, after a sensational account of the suicide of "The Napoleon of Finance," added this interesting paragraph:

The rash act is attributed to despondency, caused by the recent death of the beautiful and talented wife to whom Mr. Black was devotedly attached.

So he was dead. Really, it was a matter of absolute indifference to me. Living or dead, here or hereafter, his gross spirit could never move in that pure sphere which I already knew as heaven, and which to Esther had become an eternal home. Yet, on one point I was just a trifle curious. Could it be that this wretched nature had known the stringent ecstasy of a loyal love?

PHASE IX.

THE BEGINNINGS OF LIFE.

THE tepid sunlight of the waning afternoon bathes with tender radiance the Sacred City of the Moor. I am resting in the terraced roof garden of my boyhood's home. The world I am about to quit is beautiful to every sense. Its murmurs ascend to me tempered by distance, even as the voice of a friend softens at the prospect of parting. Below in the bazaar, the traders drone and chaffer; the camel-drivers argue with their beasts; the mule-bells tinkle. Now, from yonder minaret, a spectral muezzin hurls at mankind his warning call to prayer, and Hassan and all my Moslem household fling themselves at Mecca, face down upon the flower-gemmed roof.

"*Allah Kebar!*[53] Yea! God is very great."

The prayer is past, and Hassan is at my side again, pressing upon me fruit and cooling drink. The gathering twilight is embroidered with the scent of roses and the strains of Moorish music. Dancing girls, round-limbed and lithe, with the solace of night in their eyes, and the fever of noon in their lips, weave magic paces about my bed. The straits' blue waters quiver and flash beyond the white walls of the town. Around and about, the terraced gardens of my neighbors, gorgeous with bloom, give back to sea and sky an answering splendor. I know, as I gaze upon the grateful scene, that I may never see again, with mortal eyes, the glory of that setting sun and all the pageantry of movement, form and color that vivifies the failing day. And still, I leave it all without a qualm. For all the raptures I have named are foreign to my truer consciousness. I see and know not these appearances. I hear and give no heed to these poor echoes of earthly incident and transitory passion.

A Presence abides with me, sweet and strong, whose brilliance and loveliness put the world to shame. All music but a memory of her voice. And light itself is but the shadow cast by her surpassing purity. My Esther hovers about me through all these tedious, latter hours. Weak of limb as I am, and racked with the pains of impending dissolution, I am comforted to find that the merest breath

"The tepid sunlight...bathes with tender radiance the Sacred City"

"I am resting in the terraced roof garden of my boyhood's home."

of my familiar, keef, will now suffice to quell my dwindling sense-life and open to my spirit the vision of the Truth whose name is Beauty.[54] Yet I grow impatient for the hour and the moment, so near at hand, at last, when I shall put off for good the harness of the flesh and my soul shall stand forth, naked and undismayed forever, in that sincerer world, that universe of love and faith and fruition, where Esther dwells and waits.

The face of my good Hassan, sullen with grief, breaks cloudily in upon my brightest reveries. The dancers have ceased, and the makers of music. The watchers by my bedside whisper to one another, through tell-tale fingers, that the things I write are death-dreams, and that I have not long to live.

Fools that they are! They do not know that these are but the beginnings of life.

Bismillah! Blessed be keef.

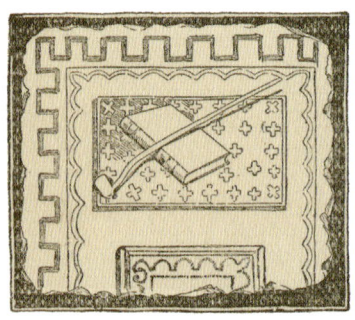

INTAGLIO PLATE CO.

Timothy Wilford Coakley.

EDITOR'S EPILOGUE

NOTE: Keef *ended with an Arabesque illustration that marked the beginning of disturbing coincidences in both this world and the fictional spiritual world. Here you may find the Arabesque promise of terror in the following recorded events.*

Timothy Wilfred Coakley, member of society, picturesque political figure and the author of *Keef,* died on February 4, 1914 in Brighton, Massachusetts. After an overcrowded funeral and mass at St. Columbkille Church, he was buried in the Holyhood Cemetery in nearby Brookline.[1] Not far away, the remains of political figures in the Kennedy family were being continually buried. And, in a burial annex at nearby Walnut Creek Cemetery, the future remains of Timothy Leary (1920–1996), another Irish author who wrote about psychedelic visions, would be initially and erroneously recorded. It turned out to be a different Timothy Leary who was actually buried there. In fact, the cremated remains of the more famous Dr. Timothy Francis Leary were hurled into space orbit by a rocket launched from a plane flying just off the coast of Morocco.[2]

The story of *Keef* opens in 1896 when the painter Leon Abecassis was dying after sending a manuscript of his memoirs to his friend Edgar Chalmers, the Theosophist, begging him to make use of the work. That memoir, albeit fictional, became the novel you have just read, and the narrator's voice is that of Abecassis. In a literary sense, Coakley, who was the real author of the memoirs, "channeled" Abecassis from the creative regions of his own brain.

Now dead at the young age of 48, Coakley could never bring Abecassis, or the other characters, back in a sequel. We are told that Leon Abecassis, a genius experimenter and fanatic believer in life after death, was dying a certain death in Tangiers at the end of the book. Most of the other main characters in the book

---

1 The Editor did not invent these names and could not have even if he tried.
2 Ashes were also distributed to Dr. Leary's family and friends.

St. Columbkille Church

Holyhood Cemetery

Walnut Street Cemetery

had been dead for several pages. Esther, Abecassis' spirit bride and *idée fixe*, passed away due to an undisclosed illness and was cremated. Her husband, Ralph Black, committed suicide. We were shown the newspaper articles to prove it. Hassan, Abecassis's faithful Sudanese servant who had rescued him from a near-death confrontation with Black, could hardly have rescued his master from the "other side" despite his tribal instincts and ritual beliefs. Indeed, the only survival possible was in the spirit world where Abecassis believed he would be united with Esther. Kif-induced visions and **"Keef Wisdom"** allowed him to see and know that this was so.[3] Chalmers, his loyal friend, silently accepted it. And it is reasonable to imagine that in this fictional world both Chalmers and Hassan, survivors of the book's original 152 printed pages, would have buried the painter in the old Jewish cemetery in Morocco, land of his boyhood. We can even picture them placing the traditional pebbles on the headstone as a mark of respect for a truly unforgettable character.

Then I was shaken by an event with the power of an earthquake! It was one of those unexpected coincidences that combine both names and likenesses and make momentary true believers of witnesses.[4] It took place in a science fiction world unimaginable in 1897. After 114 years, via a warp in space and time known

3 Mary Baker Eddy, a believer in the spiritual world who died in 1910, used morphine, which may have facilitated her "spirit communications" with her dead brother. Her drug-induced visions led to the proof as set forth in her Christian Science teachings, thereby bestowing "scientific" standing on the spirit world. Kif, like morphine, allows the vividness of the visions to be readily mistaken for veridicality, hence false visions turn truthful.

4 True believers in the supernatural, like true believers in astrology, wild conspiracy theories, or JFK-Lincoln similarities might look beyond the simple coincidence of names and numbers as mentioned here. They might find associated evidence in the uncanny similarity of looks and cite the following examples. Anna Maria Chalmers, a writer, contributed to Poe's *Southern Literary Messenger* where he published several works. Anna was married and widowed three times, died of unknown circumstances, and was buried in Richmond, Virginia where Poe spent his early years. The profile of her face, albeit aged, resembles Poe's wife as well as the woman who appears on the cover of *The New Pygmalion*. Any suggestion of a supernatural connection, however severely exaggerated, adds an amusing yet haunting footnote to Coakley's never-ending story of coincidences *par excellence*.

Old Jewish Cemetery in Marrakesh, Morocco

Anna Maria Chalmers

Virginia Poe

New Pygmalion Model

as the internet, there came a message in a bottle drifting in that digital ether. It was so shocking and terrifying that it momentarily convinced me that I had been correct all along in suspecting and, yes, hoping that there had been a special spiritual connection between Timothy Wilfred Coakley and Edgar Allan Poe—a connection I dubbed "literary channeling." Others may call it "unconscious copying" or strain to legally label it "fair use" or anything but plagiarism. Coakley's heirs might even want to retain a lawyer, perhaps his younger brother, the Hon. Daniel H. Coakley, or other law firms the family had known over the years, to defend against any postmortem charges of plagiarism.[5] While Coakley was under the influence of Poe when he wrote Abecassis' memoirs, his character creation Abecassis was also under the influence of kif. And, as happened before in the novel, the combined interaction connected him with a spiritual world. For a fleeting moment I asked myself how else could the following surprising event be explained? After all, was there not a spiritual connection between **Edgar Allan Poe** and T.W. Coakley who created the character of **Edgar Chalmers**? How would I know?

On December 16, 2011 an anonymous artist posted the following image on the internet. It was an ink and watercolour work with a most disturbing title: *Edgar Allan Chalmers*. The image haunts me still...

---

5 D.H. Coakley was removed from the Massachusetts Bar and died at age 68 from uremic poisoning in 1934 on the same day the Supreme Court denied his appeal for reinstatement. In January 1917 he donated $10,000 to Boston College in memory of his brother. Afterwards Daniel's heirs continued support for a Timothy W. Coakley Scholarship.

"Edgar Allan Chalmers"
Fall 2011

ENDNOTES

PREFACE: A WORD TO THE WISE

1 [p. 47] Since *Keef* was published in 1897, this fictional letter from Abecassis would have been written in 1896 when he mailed his attached memoirs to Chalmers. The memoirs begin in the next section of the book. The letter was postmarked from Tangiers at a time when Morocco was still an Empire ruled by a Sultan who proclaimed to be the High Priest of Islam. It was a difficult time for those of other faiths. The large Jewish population was confined to a "Hebrew Quarter" where they were subjected to many restrictions. There were violent assaults on American citizens including missionaries. An American warship stayed parked off the Bay of Tangiers. Front-page articles in American newspapers posted travel warnings. (e.g., "Empire of Morocco. Assaults on Americans May Create More Trouble," *The Pittsburg Press*, July 29, 1899). Given such stress surrounding an American of Jewish descent living in Tangiers like Abecassis, the use of legally available "medical keef" was deemed acceptable and beneficial.

2 [p. 49] This letter from Chalmers is the preface to the memoirs that will follow. As a Theosophist who believes in careful introspection and the study of psychic experiences in order to understand the metaphysical spirit world, he accepts Abecassis' pursuit of similar mystical goals. Abecassis will attempt to do so with keef and in so doing he follows the tradition of early French physicians and psychiatrists like Jacques Joseph Moreau, who followed Napoleon to Egypt and brought back hashish for his investigations. Moreau introduced it to Theophile Gautier who founded *Le Club des Haschischins* where members like Baudelaire and Gerard de Nerval described many spiritual and ecstatic experiences. Another investigator, Louis-Alphonese Cahagnet, carried out careful clinical trials with the drug and claimed that hashish visions were neither dreams nor hallucinations but actual out-of-body experiences that allowed entry into the spiritual world, thereby revealing an underlying reality. [Cahagnet, L.A. *Sanctuaire du Spiritualism*. Paris: Germer Baillière, 1850; Siegel, R.K., and A.E. Hirschman, "Hashish Near-Death Experiences." *Anabiosis*, Vol. 4, No. 1, Spring 1984, pp. 69-86. See Appendix.]

PHASE I: HOUSE OF VISIONS

3 [p. 52] Coakley's first chapter, "House of Visions," is written in the style of Edgar Allan Poe's *The Fall of the House of Usher* (1839, 1840). Coakley appears to have read many works by Poe. He was undoubtedly exposed to Poe in his education in Boston, Poe's birthplace, and at the College of Notre Dame in Baltimore where Poe lived and died. The city itself was home to the Poe House and Museum, and interestingly, the College later became home to the Edgar Allan Poe Academy. Coakley uses literary devices throughout the entire book that were originally created by Poe. In *Usher*, Poe created an unnamed narrator who receives a letter from Roderick Usher complaining of an illness and asking for help. Usher, like Coakley's narrator Abecassis, is a painter. And like Abecassis' anxiety and eventual addiction to kif, Usher is also an anxious addict, an "irreclaimable eater of opium." The Usher story was inspired by an event on Boston's Lewis Wharf, near where Coakley lived. Usher's sister Madeline, like Abecassis' Esther, becomes ill and falls into cataleptic trances. Coakley used his keef addict as a narrator just like Poe used his opium addict as a narrator for the short story "Ligeia." The "spirit bride" of Coakley's narrator falls ill with seizures and then dies just like the wife of Poe's narrator. A third source was Poe's short story "Life in Death" also known as "The Oval Portrait." The plot is uncannily identical to *Keef*. In order to avoid spoiling the ending of *Keef*, the detailed comparisons are reserved for the Editor's Epilogue and the Appendix where you will find Poe's original story in its scarce unedited form. It became Poe's shortest short story of only two pages as originally printed. It may be told at this point that all three stories mentioned here turn into horror stories at the end.

4 [p. 52] Coakley, a scholar of Catholic history and religion in general, had an appreciation for Jewish teachings and made frequent references to Hebrews and Jews in his writings and orations.

5 [p. 54] Tangiers, or Tangier, also had a slave market for European white women who were sold to the Sultans in Arabia.

6 [p. 54] Variant spellings include: hachish, hachych, hash, haschich, haschisch, hasheesh, hashish, and hatschisch.

7 [p. 54] Nepenthe is the drug described in Homer's *Odyssey* as banishing grief or trouble from a person's mind. The term can be used for any drug or potion that brings *welcomed* forgetfulness.

8 [p.54] In the name of Allah, the first phrase in the Koran, or Qur'an; an invocation used by Muslims at the beginning of any undertaking.

9 [p. 56] Artists under the influence of hallucinogens including Cannabis tend to paint outside boundaries and borders, expanding the forms, extending the lines, and embellishing the colors to reflect their enhanced feelings and altered perceptions. Concomitantly, they tend to judge their work with altered and equally inflated opinions.

10 [p. 56] For the present; an obsolete phrase.

11 [p. 58] Coakley was fluent in Spanish, traveled in Cuba and Mexico, and translated Spanish poems for Catholic magazines.

12 [p. 58] It should become apparent from the extra-illustrations in this edition that Coakley is also copying the old masters with reference to his descriptions of people and places.

PHASE II: THE SCIENCE OF INTOXICATION

13 [p. 62] In the original text Coakley spelled this word phonetically (Bhaghavad-Ghītā) as he did for several other words (e.g., grewsome) that have been corrected in this edition.

14 [p. 64] Coakley is at home when he is writing about private clubs, high society, lawyers and journalists because he moved in those circles in Boston, New York, and Los Angeles. The Siesta Club is modeled after the Union Club of New York that was located within walking distance of the types of mansions described as a residence for Abecassis. Here and elsewhere Coakley is following the rule when writing a first novel: write about what you know.

15 [p. 70] Here Coakley is providing a well-known list of drugs used by writers and artists throughout history. He was undoubtedly familiar with the names. Another even longer list can be given for writers who write about drugs rather than use them or even attempt to write, draw, or paint under the influence. Opium was the drug of choice during the romantic period that surrounded Coakley's time. Writers and poets using opium—usually in the form of laudanum—included Baudelaire, Coleridge, Wilkie Collins, Crabbe, Dickens, Keats, and Edgar Allan Poe. Poets like Charles Cros, Paul Verlaine and Arthur Rimbaud engaged in absinthe stupors at cafés yet wrote beautifully. While many artists including Manet and Picasso painted absinthe drinkers, artists like Van Gogh and Toulouse-Lautrec were always using even while painting. Toulouse-Lautrec, who liked to mix it with wine instead of water, even carried his own absinthe in a hollow cane. One of his most famous pastel portraits was Van Gogh drinking absinthe in a café in 1887, a decade before *Keef* was published. Van Gogh had just finished painting an absinthe glass and water decanter (1886), a painting that has been described as a self-portrait of the *real* Van Gogh.

16 [p. 70] The smell has been likened to dark chocolate: pleasant, soft, vegetal, and most importantly, memorable. Like other distinct aromas it only has to be detected once by the olfactory lobe in order to become imprinted in the brain. Keef in Morocco was often combined with scented or perfumed tobacco for smoking. When used while incense was burning, smoking establishments took on a characteristic identifying aroma making them easy to find in crowded commercial areas. Honey sweetened the taste as well as the smell and was sometimes added to the crushed plant parts before they were converted into hard slabs of hashish.

PHASE III: A NEW PYGMALION

17 [p. 80] The word "witchery" appears to have been taken directly from Ludlow's *The Hasheesh Eater*, the first memoirs of hashish use by an American and the first book in English on hashish. Ludlow refers to the "witch plant" and the "realm of witchery." This "witchery" description and other phrases only found in Ludlow are evidence that Coakley was familiar with the book and borrowed from it. Although the book was initially published anonymously, it created a sensation and four printings appeared in as many years. Ludlow's work also appeared in *Harper's Magazine*, a magazine probably known to Coakley. [Ludlow, Fitz Hugh. *The Hasheesh Eater; Being Passages From the Life of a Pythagorean*. New York: Harper, 1857.]

18 [p. 80] This phrase reflects remarks made about Coakley's public orations and political speeches.

19 [p. 80] An extended Benatuil family lived in Boston in 1897. Some members lived in Coakley's neighborhood and it is likely he knew this name if not individuals.

20 [p. 80] "Enslaves" is a rare and pejorative word in the literature of drug addiction despite the universal imagery of addiction and enslavement. According to the RKS Library of Drug Literature, there is only one earlier use of the word in English drug literature by an American writer, H.H. Kane (1881), a New York physician. Even the good doctor Kane, who campaigned against all drugs, had qualified the word by pointing out that some drugs like hashish did not necessarily produce enslavement or harm and may actually be of positive benefit. It is now recognized that addiction, even "enslaved" addiction, is a function of dose and pattern of use, not the drug per se. [Kane, H.H. (Harry Hubbell). *Drugs That Enslave. The Opium, Morphine, Chloral and Hashisch Habits*. Philadelphia: Presley Blakiston, 1881.]

21 [p. 82] In this section Coakley is revealing the same voice and phrases he used in his courtroom trial statements and his 1906 Fourth of July Oration in Boston.

22 [p. 82] These are the same fields of interest Coakley shared with members in private clubs in both Boston and New York. And, like experienced hashish and marijuana users, either he or his astute Abecassis discovered that recent memories shape the major contents of subsequent mental imagery in both dreams and visions while under the influence, thereby permitting a quasi-"programming" of the experience.

23 [p. 82] Refers to the lovely daughters of Israel. Tangiers was known for its large Jewish population. Drawings and paintings of the women became known as Tangerine Jewesses and decorated tourist postcards, newspapers and magazine stories.

24 [p. 84] Benjamin Constant was Coakley's favorite painter. His painting of the Jewess *Judith*, a biblical hero, was not as colorful as his major Oriental works that match many of Coakley's descriptions in this book. The painting of one of his subjects in *Harem Women* is similar to Coakley's description of Abecassis' spirit bride Esther.

25 [p. 84] Raffaele is Raffaele Giannetti, an Italian painter; Angelo is Michelangelo.

26 [p. 84] Weed was not the slang term for marijuana it is today but a common name used for hashish by most writers during this period. Ludlow used the word five times in his memoirs but early botanists and explorers were probably the first to introduce the term.

27 [p. 86] Muhammad's departure from Mecca to Medina in A.D. 622 is known as the Hegira. In the history of Islam, the Muslim era begins at this date.

28 [p. 86] Private clubs were known for their vast collections of paintings and books. Their libraries became famous for the depth of collections and elegant reading rooms. The Union League Club of New York had a strong artistic membership and art works as well. The Union Club of New York boasted of a great library and membership that included newspaper magnate William Randolph Hearst and several publishers.

29 [p. 86] There are numerous novels as well as dozens of other literary works with the word Pygmalion in the title but only one with the subtitle New Pygmalion and that was the novel *Liber Amoris: Or, The New Pygmalion*, [London: Printed for John Hunt, 1823]. Initially published as an anonymous account of a writer's foolish passion, the author has been identified as William Hazlitt who, like Coakley, was of Irish stock. The novel was inspired by the classic Ovid myth of a Cypriot goldsmith who falls in love with the statue of a woman he carved out of ivory. Hazlitt's *New Pygmalion* tells his own story of an obsessive attraction to his landlord's daughter. In his imagination he turned her into someone she was not and created imaginary conversations and letters with her. The book was released again with renewed interest in 1894, three years before Coakley's *Keef*. Coakley introduced another version but based on the Hazlitt writing. The preface in *Keef* (A Word to the Wise) with its letters describing the origin of the narrative is structured exactly like Hazlitt's preface (Advertisement) and the letters that follow. In *Keef* Abecassis comments that the book "was written with unique power," and the writer "had a rare gift of impressing the reader," all phrases that critics had written about Hazlitt. Coakley's adaptation was successful to a fault.

30 [p. 92] *Vathek* was a gothic novel by William Beckford (1782) in which the title character descends into Hell and comes upon the demon Eblis, an evil devil or jinn in Islamic literature. Vathek is doomed to wander endlessly. [Originally published without an author name as *An Arabian Tale, From an Unpublished Manuscript*, claiming to be translated from the Arabic.]

PHASE IV: PHANTASM AND FLESH

31 [p. 96] Coakley, who had blue eyes, gives Esther blue eyes, the same eyes that haunted the narrator in Poe's "The Tell-Tale Heart." Some scholars who studied Poe's portraits and daguerreotypes opined that his eyes were a bluish gray, restless, piercing, and "exhibiting a marked nervousness." The portraits of Queen Esther by Chasserua and Teichert that may have inspired Coakley had blue eyes.

32 [p. 96] Refers to Raphael Sanzio (1483–1520), an Italian Renaissance painter. His paintings were considered "divine" because they captured the very essence of the word. His self-portrait embodied the expression "Sanzio the Divine."

33 [p. 102] The Gardens of Sallust were pleasure gardens in Rome developed by Sallust, a Roman historian in the first century BC. The Goths were German tribes of huge stature who aided the fall of Rome.

34 [p. 104] The structure of this sentence reflects the organization of his written orations with the punctuation dictating the manner in which the orator spoke. This suggests that he edited the punctuation as well as the spelling by reading out loud, hence the numerous punctuated pauses and phonetically spelled words.

35 [p. 104] Here Abecassis is acknowledging that he combined alcohol and kif, a mixture that can yield a more delirious intoxication. Coakley, a drinker, could have discovered this for himself when he tried kif.

36 [p. 104] This phrase and the pages that follow create images that could be right out of Poe's best-known works: "The Tell-Tale Heart" and the poem "The Raven." In the first story the narrator is haunted by the sound of the beating heart of the old man with a "vulture eye" whom he killed. Here the narrator Abecassis is haunted by the "chill, gray eye of the ogre, Black" that ignites his heart-throbbing paranoia. In the poem Poe's narrator is haunted by a black "Raven" provided here by Ralph Black as a Raven-like stalker for narrator Abecassis. As in Poe's works, the pace here in *Keef* picks up with words evoking images of an incipient deadly end.

PHASE V: THE PASSING OF ESTHER

37 [p. 110] This questioning by Abecassis is typical of Poe's narrators.

38 [p. 112] Coakley was a member of high society and familiar with Coming Out parties for girls. He may be describing the woman he married, Elizabeth Josephine, who was at the exact same age (22) at the time he wrote the book and to whom he disguised the book's dedication.

39 [p. 114] The type of behavior described in this long paragraph is typical of pathological stalkers and sex crime offenders. The word "ravishments" suggests that sexual fantasies may have been occurring during intoxications while staring at an arousing image like Esther. Some voyeurs who might watch someone through windows at night would also masturbate in the presence of a coveted image. Such behaviors only intensify the bonding to the object of desire. In that sense Coakley has created in Abecassis a strong, scary character that is the equal of Poe's narrators. In keeping with the restraints of Coakley's Catholic upbringing, Abecassis is kept to acting no more audaciously than a peeping Tom.

40 [p. 114] Keef is derived from *Kayd*, Arabic for "delight," and use here is suggestive that feelings of kif intoxication have been conditioned to Esther's presence.

41 [p. 116] Abecassis' thoughts are consistent with the development of paranoia. Paranoid reactions to high doses of marijuana, hashish, and kif are common especially among strangers or in unfamiliar outdoor environments.

42 [p. 116] Coakley lived in a New York Madison Avenue mansion.

43 [p. 118] This was the age of American Nervousness and a disease also known as Nervous Exhaustion or Brain Exhaustion. It was an archaic diagnosis with equally archaic treatments including therapeutic coca wines containing cocaine, advertised as beneficial for waking up the exhausted brain.

44 [p. 118] Reading a book under the influence could permit the associated mental images created by the story to become imprinted. This effect was not widely mentioned in the literature of 1897 but would have been known by users who experienced it. In order to write about kif effects so accurately, Coakley may have experimented with his own use or relied on the detailed memoirs of others like Ludlow.

45 [p. 120] Withdrawal from high doses of Cannabis products including kif would not fit the descriptions here. Aside from the common effects of psychological craving, rebounding REM (dream) sleep, and hyperphagia (overeating), the effects are mild even when tobacco and wine are added. It is more likely that Abecassis is suffering from a bad case of unrequited love.

PHASE VI: ASHES TO ASHES

46 [p. 128] Colorado is Spanish for red-colored and also a slang word for a capsule containing a barbiturate tranquilizer. Since such capsules were not widely available until the 1930s, the prescription mentioned here might have referred to another medicine or perhaps a rest in the mountains of Colorado.

PHASE VII: THE ATAVISM OF HASSAN

47 [p. 144] Anak was a mixed race of giant people, reported to be taller and stronger than the Israelites, who occupied Hebron and were first mentioned in the book of Numbers.

48 [p. 146] Mussulman is an archaic term for Muslim.

49 [p. 148] *In the name of Allah* is the proper translation.

PHASE VIII: A COMMONPLACE TRAGEDY

50 [p. 152] *La Sylphide* was the name of a French Marine Nationale schooner that was launched in 1771 but was wrecked in a raid on Cayenne, the capital of French Guiana. The name proved to be unlucky and eventually spelled tragedy for any ship. Another *Sylphide* schooner pictured here was captured by the *USS Virginia* in 1861 running the Confederate blockade and later sank in a storm off the coast of Australia in 1877. *Sylphide* was also the name of a steamship built in 1848 that traveled between Boston and Liverpool. Coakley names his fictional ship *La Sylphide*, after a famous 1832 romantic ballet that tells a supernatural love story similar to *Keef*. In the ballet a Scottish farmer falls in love with a beautiful sylph, an imaginary spirit that takes the form of a forest fairy. But there is an evil witch plotting against the farmer who was to wed another. When the farmer finally turns to the sylph and holds her in a passionate embrace with the witch's scarf, her wings fall off, she shudders and then dies in his arms. He gazes heavenward and sees the sylph being carried aloft by her sister fairies. Overwhelmed by sorrow, the farmer collapses. By choosing *La Sylphide* for the ship returning Abecassis to his boyhood home in Tangiers, Coakley was providing a clue to the tragic end of the narrator/painter's own voyage. In 1904, while Coakley was touring in Russia, the Imperial Ballet was presenting a revival of the ballet with famous ballerina Anna Pavlova.

51 [p. 152] Havre is a city in the Normandy region of France.

52 [p. 152] Coakley was a journalist and newspaperman for several years and fully capable of writing a fictional newspaper article with headlines and inventing believable names like *The Daily Interviewer* or the *Morning Universe*. In fact, he wrote for Catholic papers and one was *The Universe*.

PHASE IX: THE BEGINNINGS OF LIFE

53 [p. 156] Literal translation is "God is great" or "God is the greatest."

54 [p. 158] Abecassis is self-medicating with kif thereby administering palliative care for himself (a.k.a. using **medical kif**). Terminal patients are often prescribed strong medications including synthetic Cannabis preparations as well as the natural plant products. Coakley died in 1914, the year of the Harrison Narcotics Act that regulated opiates and cocaine. His medication at the Boston City Hospital where he died is unknown. It is likely he was given an opiate like morphine for pain. Cannabis preparations remained available over the counter and would not be controlled until legislation was passed in 1934 and 1937. Smoking kif in Morocco is now illegal. Production and consumption in the Kingdom of Morocco were prohibited in 1954 but kif remains the country's largest source of foreign currency. Smoking kif continues to be popular among the indigenous male population and visiting travelers. And, yes, even modern users continue to have death-dreams when they overdose. Like Ali and other Cannabis users who take hashish or kif regularly and become addicted despite the warnings of death dreams, they dwell on thoughts that generate wild feelings despite the paranoid visions that are just around the corner. After all, seeing is believing.

Classic Depiction of a Death-Dream.
Illustration by Gottfried Sieben, *Haschisch.*
1898.

COAKLEY'S BOOKSHELF

Books With Similarities Available in 1897

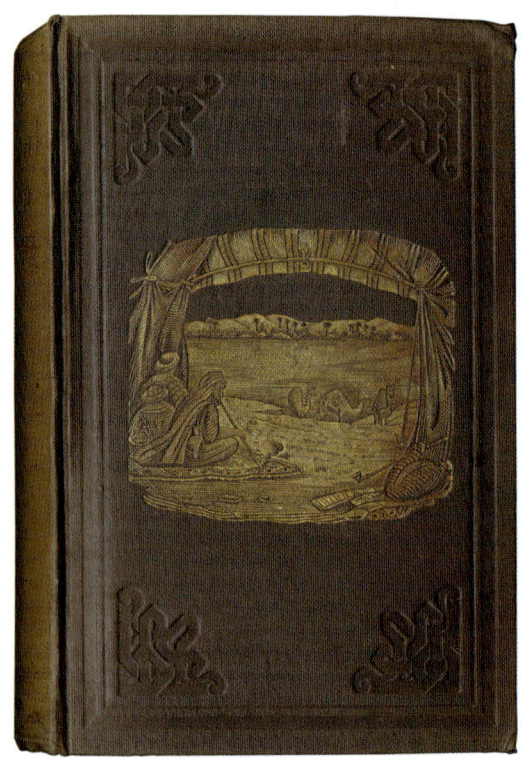

Taylor, 1854

BOOK TITLES

•[Anon.]. *Confefsions [Confessions] Of An English Hachish Eater.* London: George Redway, 1884.

•Blondel, Spire. *Le Livre des Fumerus et Des Priseurs.* Illustrations by G. Fraipont. Paris: Henri Laurens, Editeur, 1891.

•Jacolliot, Louis. *Voyage Au Pays Du Hatschisch.* Illustration De Mouillon et el Geardi. Paris: E. Dentu, Éditeur, 1883.

•King, Thorold (Ch. Gatchell). *Haschisch. A Novel.* Chicago: A.C. McClurg, 1886.

•[Ludlow, Fitz Hugh] *The Hasheesh Eater: Being Passages From The Life Of A Pythagorean.* New York: Harper & Brothers, 1857.

•Lydston, G. Frank. *Over The Hookah. The Tales Of A Talkative Doctor.* Illustrations by C. Everett Johnson. Chicago: Fred, Klein Company, 1896.

•Mangin, Arthur. *Les Poisons.* Tours: Alfred Mame et Fils, 1869. Illustrators unknown.

•Monnier, Antonine. *Hachisch. Contes En Prose. Sonnet Et Poëmes Fantaisistes.* Illustres De Trente Eaux-Fortes. Texte Et Gravures Par Antoine Monnier. Paris: Léon Eillem, Éditeur, 1877.

•Poe, Edgar Allan. *Tales And Poems Of Edgar Allan Poe, With Biographical Essay By John H. Ingram.* And Twenty Original Etchings, Five Photogravures And A New Etched Portrait. Philadelphia: George Barrie, 1895. Six Volumes. Illustrators include Chifflat, Wogel, Laurens, and Meaulle. The Oval Portrait, Vol. 2. Illustration by J.F. Laurens. (c. 1884).

•Prime, William C. *Boat Life In Egypt And Nubia.* New York: Harper & Bros., 1857. Illustrators unknown.

•Taylor, Bayard. *Journey To Central Africa; Or Life And Landscapes From Egypt To The Negro Kingdoms Of The White Nile.* New York: G.P. Putnam & Co., 1854. Illustrations by Bayard Taylor.

•Taylor, Bayard. *The Lands Of The Saracen; Or, Pictures Of Palestine, Asia Minor, Sicily, And Spain.* New York: G.P. Putnam & Co.; London: Sampson Low, Son & Co., 1855. Illustrations by Bayard Taylor.

INSIDE THE BOOKS
Similarities to *Keef*

From: ***Boat Life in Egypt and Nubia* by W.C. Prime, 1857.**

In a chapter entitled "Visions and Realities" Prime describes his personal experience with kif that he claims is superior to his many experiences with tobacco smoking and beer drinking. In *Keef*, Abecassis finds his kif experiences superior to alcohol and other drugs. Prime, like Coakley, writes about the blue fumes of smoke; seems fixated by blue eyes; and longs for his boyhood home. Both authors express similar awe and feelings for the newfound experiences. Prime's visions included dreams with "out- 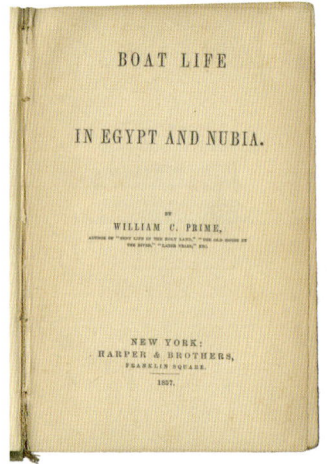 lines of fair and gentle persons in the air, delicate outlines of rare beauty. There were blue eyes gazing out... on me. ....I could have rested there a century in that delicious kief, that no man may know in any other spot on earth....There is no spot on all the world's surface to which I look back with a memory of such perfect calm delight, such undisturbed re- pose of mind and body as the shop-front ...in the bazaar [where he obtained the kief]." (pp. 454–455).

Prime goes on to relate a story he heard on his travels about Selim Pasha, governor of Upper Egypt under Mohammed Ali. It was a romance in a harem wherein Selim chooses a girl for his bride who was seen in a dream, with the voice he heard in a dream and the blue eyes that so bewildered him. When he lifts up her veil "it was so gloriously beautiful. Her forehead was white as the forehead he saw when he did dream...and her eyes were bluer and deeper than the sky...The brown hair rolled back like a river of jewels from her splendid head, and her lips" (p. 457). Abecassis' reaction to his spirit bride Esther bears a strong resemblance to Prime's storied dream bride.

The author describes eating hashish, which he found too bitter and combined it with a sweet Turkish confection. He became a user in order to be in a place called "Keef" that the author defined as the Arab state of delight: "It often follows upon periods of great mental excitement, and may be described as a feeling of immense and illimitable calm, of sublime spiritual elevation, and of complete liberation from the trammels of the flesh. The true body seems to painlessly shrivel and shrink off, leaving nothing but a kind of lingo sharira, or astral body, which is transparent and imponderable....one of the most delightful of experiences." (pp. 14–15).

He also describes a vision of "a divinely lovely sylph" that he kept looking for in his Keef dreams: "I had no aim save love. I thought only of her" (p. 18) in the same way Esther seduced Abecassis in his dream world. Consequently Abecassis describes his aim for Esther "in the cause of keef and love." Here the anonymous author, like Abecassis, turns the quest into a real romance that ends in tragedy and the death of his beloved.

Along the way, the author of this memoir, which qualifies as a "**Plot Twin**" for Coakley's novel, has nightmare visions of a serpent, the harbinger of death, in the Eden of Keef. While he falls in love and unites with her, she dies in Edgar Alan Poe style: "Look at the gallows there. Look at the Raven! How he caws!" (p. 27). This parallels Coakley words: "In a spiritual Eden I wandered hand in hand with the fairest of womankind." (*Keef*, p. 52). And here he feels like Vathek in the Halls of Eblis, a literary image of descending into Hell and coming upon a demon or devil.

From: _Haschisch. A Novel_ by Thorold King [Ch. Gatchell], 1886.
This book went through five editions: three by A.C. McClurg in Chicago (1886) and two by Brentano's in New York (1888). There were rave reviews, especially in all the Boston newspapers and magazines. Indeed, copies of the Boston reviews were pasted into a book as a frontispiece along with reviews from Chicago, Cincinnati, New Orleans, New York, Philadelphia, St. Louis, even Paris. The _Atlantic Monthly_ wrote: 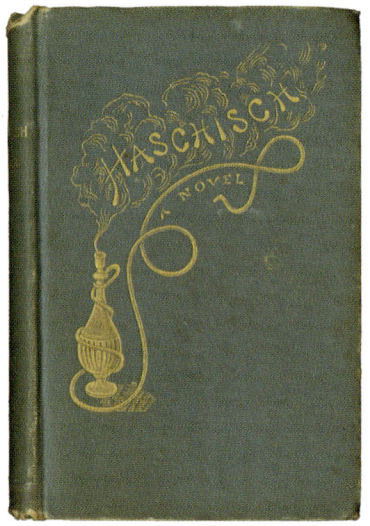 "Haschisch is a sensational story in which the drug plays a marvelous part." Other reviewers called attention to a cleverly constructed story of love and romance mixed with a tragic theme—haschisch. The structure of a novel with the drug playing the title character role is so similar to _Keef_, which appeared nine years later, it seems likely Coakley was aware of the book. Like _Keef_, it begins with a "wise word" and midway through the book the narrator describes his introduction to haschisch as a strange experience with fantastic visions and compares them to a famous painting: "I remember seeing, driving across the sky, like Guido's _Aurora Rospigliosi_, an endless procession of immense chariots, and to me each one represented a century of time" (p. 231). This particular comparison is uncannily similar to Abecassis, the _Keef_ narrator, who was always making comparisons with great works of art. There are enough other strong similarities in descriptions and plot between _Keef_ and _Haschisch_ that King's earlier novel can be listed as one of the likely fiction sources for Coakley in addition to Edgar Allan Poe's short stories including _Life in Death/ The Oval Portrait_.

The "Kif" Cigarette, James Henderson Postcard: London, c.1899–1910

LIST OF ILLUSTRATIONS

Page 53
•Carte Postale. Tanger-Maroc. Panorama Nord. Au Grand Paris: Nahon & Lasry, Tanger (Maroc).
•Carte Postale. Roofs of Tangier From the British Consulate, Showing Flagstaffs of Foreign Legations. Italian legation is at the center of the photograph. Cavilla, Photo, Tangier.

Page 55
•Carte Postale. Tanger (Maroc). Porte de la Ville. Au Grand Paris: Nahon et Lasry, Tanger (Maroc).
•Carte Postale. Tangier. Camels at Soko.
•Postcard. Farmer, Rif Mountains, Morocco. ©Peter One, c. 1975.

Page 57
•Carte Postale. Tanger. Le Petit Sokko.
•*Arabs in an Interior (At the Bazaar)* by Benjamin Constant (1845–1902).
•Engraving by Gustave Fraipont (1849–1923), in *Le Livre des fumerus et Des Priseurs* by Spire Blondel. Paris: Henri Laurens, 1891. [Original caption: "Pipes intersect so we must be careful not to break his teeth."]

Page 59
•Engraving by Gustave Fraipont, in Blondel, 1891. [Original caption: "In summer, sitting under a tree, a Muslim lights his pipe."]
•Postcard. Roma. Ponte Vittorio Emaneule II.

Page 61
•Detail from the fresco *Assumption of the Virgin* by Antonio da Correggio (1489–1534), 1522–30.
•Detail from *The Wedding at Cana* by Paolo Veronese (1528–1588). 1562–63.
•*Les Pèlerins d'Emmaüs* by Rembrandt Harmenszoon van Rijn, (1606-1669), 1629.

Page 63
•Detail from *Selling Flowers on a Roman Street* by Raffaele Giannetti (1832–1916).
•*The Entry of the Animals into Noah's Ark* by Jan Brueghel the Elder (1568–1625), 1613.
•*Two Old Men Eating Soup (or The Witchy Brew)* by Francisco José de Goya y Lucientes (1746–1828), c. 1819–23.

•Competitive Design for the Union Club-House, New York by Donn Barber, Architect, n.d.
•Members of the Union League Club, New York, 1903.

Page 67
•Engraving by Gustave Fraipont, in Blondel, 1891. [Original caption: "I want to support and not break teeth, It is only a pipe with tobacco in it."]

Page 69
•*The Watchful Guard.* Painting by Benjamin Constant (1845–1902), 1873.

Page 71
•Tobacco store in Watertown, New York, c. 1890s. Photograph by Horace E. Wait.

Page 73
•*The Rug Merchant.* Painting by Frederick Arthur Bridgman (1847-1928).

Page 75
•Illustration by Miranda. Frank Leslie's *Historical Register of the U.S. Centennial Exposition in Philadelphia in 1876 and New York, 1877.* Also printed by Fitz Hugh Ludlow Memorial Library Note Cards, ©1974. [Original caption: "American Visitors Smoking Chibouques in the Turkish Bazaar."]

[**TWIN NOTE:** Both images have three figures in similar positions. There are round tables, pipes, and a similar arrangement of furniture. Abecassis is on the divan while the twin is slouched in a similar position and wearing the same suit. The twin's long thin legs are similar to Abecassis' here as well as on page 124 where he appears to be wearing the same shoes as the twin. The hair and facial features are almost identical except for the aging on the twin. If Ritchie was copying the twin, he probably found it easy to copy a similar posture, keeping the left side of the face, bent left leg and elbow, and right hand holding the pipe.]

Page 77
•Postcard. Tanger, Maroc. Grand Sokko.
•Postcard. Port of Tangier, Morocco.
•Postcard. New York, The Wonder City.

Page 79
•Illustration of Haschisch Dreams by Gottfried Sieben (1856–1918), 1898. From *Haschisch: An Oriental Legend* by Fritz Lemmermeyer. Budapest: Verlag von Gustav Grimm, 1898.

• Engraving by Gustave Fraipont, in Blondel, 1891. [Original caption: "A forerunner of the delights promised by the prophet's all good servant of Islam."]

•*Jewish Woman from Tangiers (Juive de Tanger)* by Charles Zacharie Landelle (1821–1908).
•*An Arab Encampment* by Charles-Théodore Frère (1814–1888), French Orientalist painter.

•Illustrator unknown. In *Boat Life in Egypt and Nubia* by William C. Prime, 1857. [Original caption: "Sheik Houssein Ibn-Egid."]

•Cover of *Liber Amoris: or, The New Pygmalion* by William Hazlitt (1778-1830). Dodo Press Edition: Boston. The woman on the cover was a model for painter John William Waterhouse (1849–1917).

•Trade Card. Advertisement for P. Rolland Nouveautés. Illustrator unknown.

•Tarjeta Postal Card. Peaton arabe Tanger: Benzaquen & Co., c. 1873.

[**TWIN NOTE:** Keeping the similarity of posture is good evidence that Ritchie may have used the twin as a model. Ritchie's Hassan is facing in the same direction with similar, albeit more hairy, muscular arms. The images share similar bulky figures, facial hair, and headdress. Ritchie's Hassan also shares similar features with his Sudanese counterparts in several Oriental paintings including *The Watchful Guard* by Benjamin Constant on page 69.]

•*The Spirit of "Haschisch"* by Sidney Herbert Sime (1867–1941). Appeared in "Haschisch Hallucinations" by H.E. Gowers. In *The Strand Magazine*, July 1905.

•Illustration by C. Everett Johnson in *Over the Hookah. The Tales of a Talkative Doctor* by G. Frank Lydston. Chicago: Fred, Klein Company, 1896. Illustration for a poem about a smoker's visions and passions.

Page 97
•*La Toilette d'Esther* by Theodore Chasseriau (1819–1856), 1841.
•Detail from *Queen Esther* by Minerva Teichert (1888–1976), 1939.

Page 99
•Illustration by Bayard Taylor in *Journey to Central Africa: Or Life and Landscapes from Egypt to the Negro Kingdoms of the White Nile* by Bayard Taylor. New York: G.P. Putnam & Co., 1854.

Page 101
•Tobacco Shop, 1890. Illustration by Gustave Fraipont in Blondel, 1891.

Page 103
•Interior Room of Astor Mansion.
•*Penitent St. Mary Magdalene* by Tiziano Vecelli or Titian (1485–1576). 1560-65.
•*The Church at Greville* by Jean-Francois Millet (1814–1875). 1871–74.
•*Evening Landscape (The Ferryman Evening)* by Jean-Baptiste Camille Corot (1796–1875), 1839.

Page 105
•Title page illustration by Antonine Monnier in *Hachisch. Contes en Prose. Sonnet et Poëmes Fantaisistes* by Antonine Monnier. Paris: Léon Eillem, Éditeur, 1877.

Page 107
•*Portrait of Madame Hélène Vincent* by Benjamin Constant (1845–1902). 1893.

[**TWIN NOTE:** Notice Ritchie's Esther: the hair, neck, long arms, and seemingly tall shapely figure in a modest but long gown. Imagine turning her around and you will find the twin in Benjamin Constant's painting. Furthermore, the silken gold hair, red lips, and queenly radiant appearance fit Coakley's descriptions but lack the blue eyes seen in other portraits of Queen Esther on page 97.]

Page 109
•Illustration by C. Everett Johnson in Lydston, 1896. Illustration of a satirical anti-smoking poem wherein freedom from care and contentment for the mind will end with gossip with a skeleton.

Page 111
•Postcard. Illustration by Cobb Shinn, c. 1909. ©E.B. Scofield.

Page 113
•Caption: Ecstatic rest of the Orient. By Gustave Fraipont, in Blondel, 1891.

Page 115
•Caption: The savage is occupied with only smoking his pipe. By Gustave Fraipont, in Blondel, 1891.

Page 117
•John Jacob Astor. From the drawing by Pierre Morand made November 12, 1842.
•Astor Mansion.

Page 119
•Caption: Haschischins in the House of the Lord of the Mountain. Illustrator unknown. In *Les Poisons* by Arthur Mangin. Tours: Alfred Mame et Fils, 1869.

Page 121
•Caption: We do not see a Turk or Arab without his pipe. By Gustave Fraipont, in Blondel, 1891.

Page 123
•Queen Victoria's Funeral Train, February 1901.

Page 125
•Repeat. By Gustave Fraipont, in Blondel, 1891.

Page 127
•Caption: In the Orient, men, women, children smoke at all times of the day. By Gustave Fraipont, in Blondel, 1891.

Page 129
•Caption: Ancient Cedars in the Forest of Lebanon. Title Page illustration by Bayard Taylor, in *The Lands of the Saracen: Or, Pictures of Palestine, Asia Minor, Sicily, and Spain* by Bayard Taylor. New York: G.P. Putnam & Co., London: Sampson Low, Son & Co., 1855.

Page 131
•Caption: An Arab presents him an engraved pipe. By Gustave Fraipont, in Blondel, 1891.

Page 133
•*Jewess of Tangiers* in *Frank Leslie's Sunday Magazine,* January 1883. Based on *A Jewess of Tangiers*, lithograph by Eugene Delacroix (1798–1863), c. 1832.

Page 135
•*The Oval Portrait* by J.P. Laurens, c. 1894; in Poe, 1895.

Page 137
•John Jacob Astor III, 1890.

[**TWIN NOTE:** Coakley describes Ralph Black as a Wall Street rail-road wrecker having an elephantine way, giving sumptuous dinners, a connoisseur of paintings, and wearing a voluminous topcoat. Ralph Black lives in a large mansion with countless rooms, one of which is for showing his priceless art collection. Such descriptions fit John Jacob Astor III in almost every way. Ritchie's Black is drawn with the same bulk, topcoat, and trademark sideburns as the twin Astor showing the stolid face, colossal shape, and superior bulk. While Ritchie's Ralph Black is always standing (pages 66 and 96) and there were a few old sketches of Astor in other positions, it was this popular 1890 sketch that tells us that both Coakley and Ritchie must have had John Jacob Astor III in mind while creating the character of Ralph Black. In support of that conclu-sion, the Astor mansion and art room were used in extra-illustrations when referring to Ralph Black. The John Jacob Astor (opium smuggler and fur trader) stalking Abecassis on page 77 was one of the many As-tor relatives that carried the same name and was used because an image of John Jacob Astor III standing could not be found. Nonetheless, it is reasonable to conclude that Ralph Black was John Jacob Astor III.]

Page 139
•Illustration by Bayard Taylor, in Taylor, 1854.

Page 141
•Caption: Modern Oriental Costume. Frontispiece by Bayard Taylor, in Taylor, 1854.

Page 143
•Illustration by Bayard Taylor, in Taylor, 1855.

Page 145
•Illustration by C. Everett Johnson in Lydston, 1896. Illustration for a racial poem humiliating smokers like this man who is sitting with crossed legs and smoking a hookah.

Page 147
•Carte Postale. Egypte. Guerriers Soudanais.

Page 149
•Illustration by Bayard Taylor, in Taylor, 1855.

Page 151
•Caption: As soon as a ship is signaled arriving from Cuba. Engraving by Gustave Fraipont, in Blondel, 1891.

APPENDIX

POEMS
by T.W. Coakley

Mount Parnassus, painting by Edward Dodwell, 1821.

In ancient Greek mythology this mountain was the home of the Muses and became known as the home of poetry, as well as the homes of music and literature. The French called it *Mont Parnasse* and Coakley identified with a French school of poetry known as Parnassian. When he saw the painting, he named Edward Dodwell his favorite Irish painter.

The authorial inscription reads in full: *"My Dear Michael Ward, my boyhood's chum at college, to whom I owe my introduction to the vistas vouchsafed only to those who have learned to love and follow the Parnassian climbers, and to whom I owe a boon more precious still—the friendship of a friend indeed. With deep delight, I subscribe myself—Yours as in the old days, Timothy Wilfred Coakley."*

NOTE: Coakley inscribed a copy of *Keef* to Michael F. Ward, a Boston College chum whom he met in French class in 1878–79. Ward introduced him to Parnassian, the French school of poetry. The Parnassians, headed by Théophile Gautier, known for his hashish and opium poetry, stressed restraint, objectivity, technical perfection, and precise description as a reaction against the emotion and excess of Romanticism. Gautier's famous Hashish Club (*Club des Haschischins*) was a literary group dedicated to experimenting with Cannabis. While Coakley's poetry is representative of the Parnassian emphasis on metrical form rather than emotion, his writing in *Keef* is representative of precise description of the drug-induced effects and visions without excessive emotion. He joined other "Parnassian climbers" who followed this path yet he took it to new literary heights where the details of kif dreams and visions became woven together into a love story with a profound, albeit underlying, Gothic emotion.

THE COLLEGE BEAUTIFUL.

BY TIMOTHY WILFRED COAKLEY, '84.

Because fact is born of vision, because faith
    makes all things whole,
We have prayed that our eyes be single and
    swerve not from the goal.
Look! On the grass-clad hilltop, where chestnut
    and maple blow,
And the groping elm-trees yearn to the mother-
    green below,
Embodied in marble and granite, throned on the
    lake's clear blue,
Real as the sky and the sunshine, the Dream
    that we dared is come true.

It is builded, our stately cloister, where Wisdom
    makes her home.
The stem-like columns flower into arch and sculp-
    tured dome,
The pillared halls are vaulted and lofty like the
    night,
And each embrasured window is a rose of rain-
    bow light.
Behold the court of science, and yonder the house
    of art;
And higher yet, God's altar, aflame with the
    Sacred Heart.

Here Goodness, Truth and Beauty are wor-
    shipped as one, not three,
And Faith companions Reason; and Order, Lib-
    erty.

Here echoes the mystic Word which only the
    angels ken;
Here beckons a Light to the Gentiles. The
    Rabbi is teaching again.
The children of men are patterned on a God self-
    sacrificed,
And the circle of life is centered and squared on
    the Cross of Christ.

In the glowing forge of boyhood, tomorrow is
    wrought today.
What we think in our hearts, we shall be, we
    create when we dream or pray.
So we pay our debt to the future, that righteous-
    ness may not cease;
Humanity here is drilled to fight for the Prince
    of Peace.

Soldiers, equipped, alert, mount guard at the
Gate of Truth,
The Company of Jesus, the living fort of youth.
Scholars are they and priests, yet ever, and fore
most, chums;
For goodly and great is learning, but love can
solve all sums.
And these serve under Him Whom only love can
reach,
And Who came as a friend to friends, since only
a friend can teach.

Loyola, we bring by the million recruits for the
war you plan.
God's Laity marches behind you.   Hear the long
acclaim of our clan;
We are the stone of the corner, the body of be-
lief.
We rear college and altar.   *We* are the world's
relief.
Saints and martyrs and sages, prelates and pon-
tiffs all
They are the answers we offered when we heard
the Master call.
Patriarch, prophet and psalmist, to each our
lines we trace.
Flesh of our flesh is the beauty that was Mary's
virgin face.
Ours is the flock and fold of the spotless Lamb of
God;
We gave to Christ the blood that drenched Gol-
gotha's sod.

Life gives and is given forever to foil the miser,
Death.
Love is the price of living and breath is spent
for breath.
What yet may we give, dear Lord, that is worthy
in Thy sight?
In Thy name, all we have, all we are, we proffer
our College tonight.
Lord, hear the prayer of Thy people.   At Thy
heart we have kindled a star.
Let its radiance grow in the darkness 'til all
men sight it afar
And are drawn to the Flame that feeds it, to
the Light the world has lacked,
And the shadows pass and the semblance and we
face the Eternal Fact.

Longfellow and Emerson.

Twin suns that long illumed this land of ours,
Gilding the weary paths in which we plod
With rays of poesy, and from the sod .
Of cold and sordid hearts alluring flowers
Of fair philosophy, have set; and o'er us lowers
The dark.   And though a tearful trust in God
Upheld us while as yet the bright ones trod
The west of life and fashioned fairy bowers
From cloud-banks by the magic of a glow,
Then potent even as at highest noon,
The aching breast *now* every balm defies
Of consolation;—now we fear to know
The falling night, and can but sit and croon:
" Ah!   When will two such other suns arise?"

T. W. COAKLEY.

Santa Teresa.

There is a fire from which the human soul,
Asbestos-like, comes whole and purified;
A Magdalen, an instant burnt, outvied
Chaste anchorites in rigid self-control:
And, on the hill of Calvary, the goal
That waits the good was pledged to him who cried,
—Thief though he was—for mercy, where, beside
His tortured God, he hung in bitter dole.
What wonder that Teresa, mystic saint,
Whose breast, a furnace of God's love, was fanned
From infancy to age to a white heat
By angel wings, knew not an earthly taint,
And went before her Maker's judgment-seat
As pure as when created by His hand!

T. W. COAKLEY, '83.

LOVE.

(Attributed to St. Francis Xavier, and recited daily by St. Ignatius of Loyola before his crucifix.)

'Tis not the heaven which Thou hast promised me.
  Dear God, that makes me love Thee as I do;
  It is not hell—and yet I fear it too—
That makes me dread the thought of vexing Thee:
'Tis thine own Self, Lord, tortured on that Tree,
  Nailed to that Cross; 'tis all the woe I view,
  The many shames Thy wounded body knew,
The thirst and throes of Thy death-agony.

  Thy love so wins me that—Christ hear my vow—
  Were there no heaven, I'd hold Thee no less dear;
  Were there no hell, yet Thee, Lord, I should fear:
  I need no bribe—I'd love Thee anyhow;
  Much as I hope, were I quite hopeless here,
  I still should love Thee as I love Thee now.

From the Spanish by

TIMOTHY WILFRED COAKLEY.

COAKLEY FAMILY SCRAPBOOK

News for Timothy's Birthday, May 10, 1865

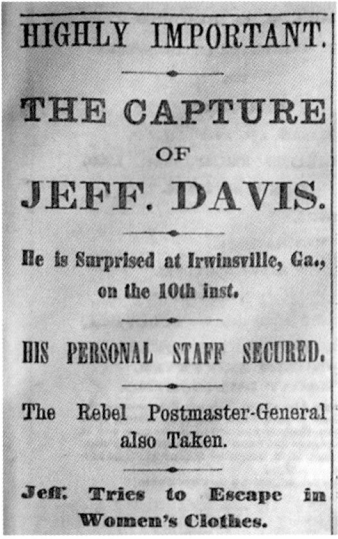

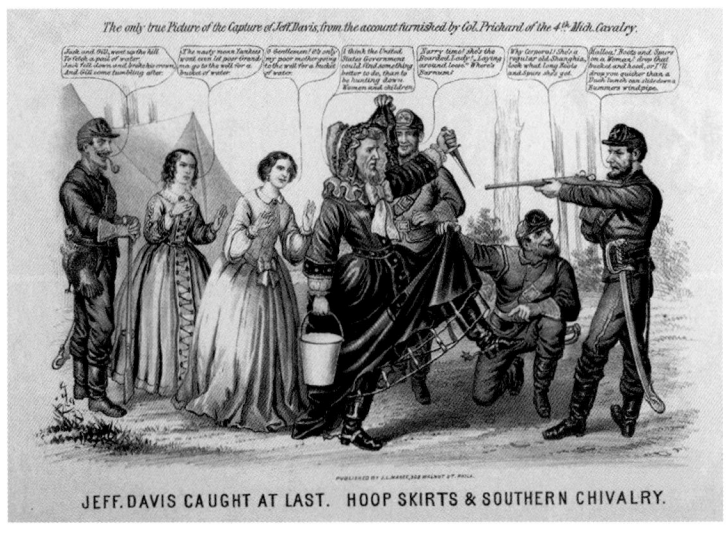

LITERARY EVENING.

JUNE 29.

SHAKESPEARE'S FIVE-ACT TRAGEDY.

KING JOHN.

JOHN, KING OF ENGLAND	J. J. Moore.
Prince Henry, his son	T. W. Coakley.
Prince Arthur, his nephew	J. A. Walsh.
Lord Constant, tutor of Arthur (substituted for Constance)	J. W. McCormack.
Earl of Pembroke	J. H. Rockwell.
Earl of Essex	M. J. Moore.
Earl of Salisbury	W. P. Cashman.
Robert Bigot	J. J. Downey.
Hubert	M. R. McCarthy.
Faulconbridge	J. P. Murphy.
Robert Faulconbridge	J. I. McLaughlin.
James Gurney, steward to the Faulconbridges	F. E. Fletcher.
Peter of Pomfret	C. V. Carroll.
English Herald	D. S. Harkins.
English Knight	J. E. McCafferty.
Executioner	M. J. Corbett.
Citizen of Angiers	F. E. Carroll.
Philip, King of France	W. F. Powers.
Lewis, the Dauphin	J. H. Carney.
Archduke of Austria	J. F. Aylward.
Lord Pandulph	J. V. Tracy.
Melun	F. J. Cunningham.
Chatillon, French ambassador	E. N. Manning.
French Herald	J. P. Quinn.

Lords, Knights, Officers, Pages, Standard-Bearers, Soldiers, etc.

Coakley as Prince Henry in Shakespeare's *King John*, 1881

COAKLEY—SMITH.

Wedding Was One of Brilliance and Largely Attended.

The most fashionable wedding of the season in Roxbury took place at St Patrick's church, Mt Pleasant, yesterday morning.

Timothy Wilfred Coakley of Brighton and Miss Elizabeth Jane, daughter of Felix Smith of 72 Blue Hill av, were married in the presence of one of the largest gatherings ever present in the edifice.

The strains of a wedding march, played by Prof Edward J. MacGoldrick, organist of the church, announced the coming of the bridal party shortly after 9 o'clock.

The ushers, Messrs Charles A. Smith, J. T. Hughes, E. A. McCarthy, J. J. Hannon, J. M. Dennison and F. P. McManus, led the way. Then followed the maid of honor, Miss May Smith, sister of the bride.

The bride, leaning upon the arm of her father, came next. Miss Agnes Conkley, sister of the groom, was bridesmaid, and brought up the rear of the procession.

At the chancel rail they were met by the groom and his best man, who was Dr F. J. Barnes of Cambridge.

Rev Fr Aiken performed the ceremony, celebrating a nuptial mass. Rev Frs Brosnahan and Thomas Walsh were present.

The music was especially grand. Weber's mass in G was sung by the choir, and the processional and recessional marches were from Theodore Dubois' nuptial mass. At the offertory Joseph S. Judge rendered Millard's "Ave Vorum." The quartet comprised Miss Katherine L. Noas, soprano, Miss Jennie E. McCann alto, Joseph S. Judge tenor and Thomas A. Jennings basso.

The quartet was as listed by Misses Minnie O'Connor, Mary Kelley, Mary McCarthy, Helen Dugan, Margaret Foley and Mabel Hennessey.

The bride is a strikingly pretty girl of the brunette type, and is extremely popular in Roxbury society. She wore a gown of white duchess satin, trimmed with lace and the usual tulle veil, caught up with lilies of the valley. She carried an ivory covered prayer book, studded with pearls. Her only ornament was a diamond pendant, the gift of the groom.

The bridesmaid was attired in dotted swiss muslin, trimmed with a garland of violets. She wore a ribbon toque and carried a bunch of violets. The maid of honor wore pink silk with hat to match, and carried a basket of pink roses.

After the ceremony the bridal party repaired to the home of the bride's father, 72 Blue Hill av, where a reception was held. Mr and Mrs Coakley received their guests in the front parlor, and many were the congratulations showered upon them.

The floral decorations were profuse and elaborate. In a large room the numerous wedding gifts, which were of a costly and handsome nature, were displayed to advantage. An elaborate wedding breakfast was served.

Mr and Mrs Coakley will pass their honeymoon in the South and upon their return will reside on Eldora st, Brookline.

Boston Daily Globe, February 6, 1894

New Books.

Keef: A Life Story in Nine Phases.

In the romance with the above named title, Timothy Wilfred Coakley, the well known lawyer and public man, has entered upon a new field of mental effort, in which he shows unusual talent as a writer of fiction. His pages betray a brilliant imagination and a facile descriptive faculty, and his style is picturesque without being overladen with ornament. The hero is an artist, a native of Tangiers, Morocco, who has some remarkable psychical experiences, through the use of the drug called keef, a Moorish preparation of Indian hemp, which in its essential principle, we are told, is identical with the hasheesh of the Turks and the majoon of Calcutta. The plot of the tale is very slight, but it is sufficient to hold together the remarkable incidents disclosed. As a work of art the book is exceedingly clever, but we have no great liking for books that describe the peculiar dreams produced by narcotics and stimulants. De Quincey's "Confessions of an Opium Eater" did more harm than good, and though the present book is only a romance, we could have wished that Mr. Coakley had exercised his undoubted literary ability upon some other subject. The volume is handsomely bound and illustrated, and is published by Charles E. Brown & Co., Boston. The price is $1.00.

First Review of *KEEF*
The Sacred Heart Review,
June 19, 1897

The firm have sent Mr. Timothy Wilfred Coakley, a well-known Boston lawyer, very prominent in the last presidential campaign, to the Philippines for a trip of exploration to be converted into exploitation when he returns. They expect great things from Coakley on the Philippines.

The Bookseller,
Newsdealer and
Stationer,
September 15, 1898

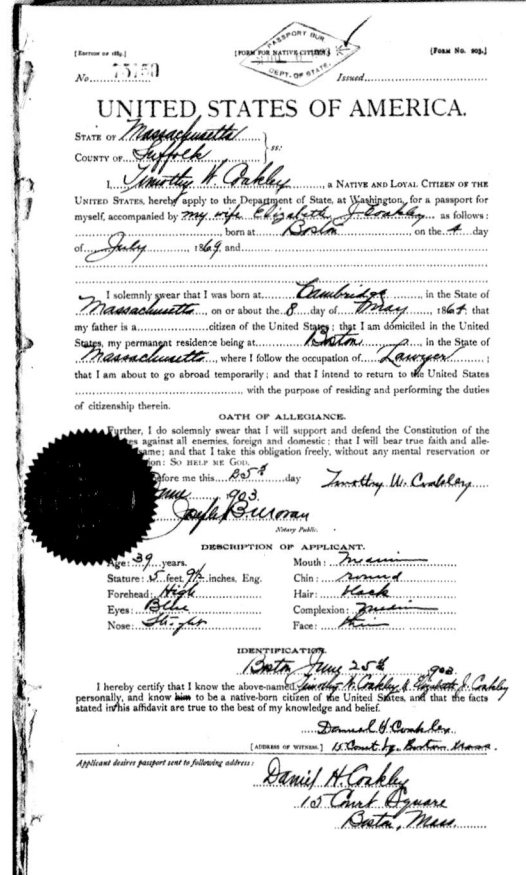

Passport Application for
Timothy and Elizabeth,
June 25th, 1903

Timothy Wilfred Coakley, who has been ill for several weeks, accompanied by Mrs. Coakley and Miss Mary Margaret Smith, Mrs. Coakley's sister, left Boston for New York yesterday to sail for Liverpool on the Cunarder Campania. The party has planned an extensive tour of the British Islands, France, Germany, Italy, Switzerland, Russia and Algiers, returning home late in September via Naples and the Azores.

Ship Souvenir
Card,
August 1912

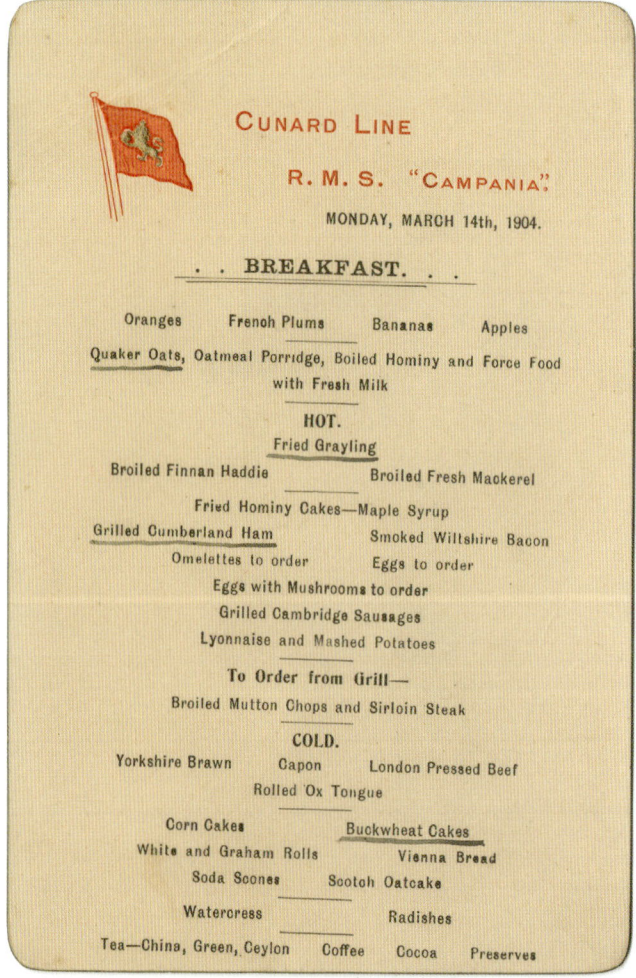

Ship Breakfast
Menu,
March 14, 1904

CUNARD LINE

R. M. S. "CAMPANIA".

MONDAY, MARCH 14th, 1904.

. . BREAKFAST. . .

Oranges   Frenoh Plums   Bananas   Apples

Quaker Oats, Oatmeal Porridge, Boiled Hominy and Force Food
with Fresh Milk

HOT.

Fried Grayling

Broiled Finnan Haddie   Broiled Fresh Mackerel

Fried Hominy Cakes—Maple Syrup

Grilled Cumberland Ham   Smoked Wiltshire Bacon

Omelettes to order   Eggs to order

Eggs with Mushrooms to order

Grilled Cambridge Sausages

Lyonnaise and Mashed Potatoes

To Order from Grill—

Broiled Mutton Chops and Sirloin Steak

COLD.

Yorkshire Brawn   Capon   London Pressed Beef

Rolled Ox Tongue

Corn Cakes   Buckwheat Cakes

White and Graham Rolls   Vienna Bread

Soda Scones   Scotch Oatcake

Watercress   Radishes

Tea—China, Green, Ceylon   Coffee   Cocoa   Preserves

WEDDED TEN YEARS.

Many Friends with Mr and Mrs Timothy W. Coakley.

Friends to the number of 200 thronged the home of Mr and Mrs Timothy W. Coakley at 374 Arborway, Jamaica Plain, last night, to congratulate them on the 10th anniversary of their marriage, and also to welcome Mr Coakley, who returned Saturday from an extended tour of the southern states, Cuba and Mexico Mingled with congratulations for husband and wife were felicitations to Mr Coakley on his restoration to health by his trip.

A number of the guests took part in an impromptu musical entertainment and after supper addresses were made and many tokens of the good will of their friends were presented to Mr and Mrs Coakley.

Boston Globe,
April 4, 1904

Fourth of July Oration,
July 4, 1906

COAKLEY PUT OUT OF COURT

Well-Known Lawyer and Politician Ejected by Order of Judge Bond in the First Jury Session of the Superior. Court—An Un- precedented Event in Court Circles

An unprecedented action in court circles took place at 3.30 o'clock yesterday after- noon, when Deputy Sheriff William W. Campbell was ordered by Judge Bond, in the first jury session of the Superior Court, to eject from the courtroom Timothy Wil- fred Coakley, a well-known lawyer and politician. A few minutes later, however, Mr. Coakley was allowed to return, but just before the Court adjourned Mr. Coakley again had trouble with the judge, and the latter ordered the crier to adjourn the court while Mr. Coakley was still talking.

The episode occurred during the trial of the suit of Annie Davis against the Boston Elevated Railway Company, in which the plaintiff seeks damages for personal injuries received on Nov. 10, 1899, by an explosion from the electrical apparatus on a car on which she was a passenger. Mr. Coakley and Herbert L. Baker appear as counsel for the plaintiff and George H. Mellen and A. I. Peckham for the defendant. Henry M. Ballard, superintendent of the construction and equipment department of the road, was called to the stand for the defence, and he began to testify from certain records in a book, when counsel for the plaintiff raised a question as to their admissibility in that form.

Judge Bond asked the witness to allow him to look at the book, and Mr. Ballard showed it to the Court, at the same time explaining certain matters. He spoke in such a low tone that what he was saying was not intelligible to the counsel, and Mr. Coakley interposed a suggestion to the wit- ness that if he had anything to say while on the stand he should say it so the Court, counsel and jury could hear it. His honor felt that the interruption was unnecessary, since he was simply asking the witness to point out something which he did not think it necessary the jury should hear.

Mr. Coakley insisted that jury and coun- sel should hear everything said on the stand, and His Honor remarked that the witness should repeat what he had told the Court. Mr. Coakley said he did not care to have the witness repeat what he had said to the Court, but simply made the suggestion with reference to the future.

"First you ask to have it, and then you don't want it," said Judge Bond, and Mr. Coakley asked leave to explain, but the Court did not wish to hear him talk.

"Go back and sit down," said the judge, and Mr. Coakley said he should obey the instructions of the Court, and sat down. In an instant he was on his feet and said now that he had obeyed the instructions of the Court he arose to ask that an exception be noted to the remark of the Court order- ing him to sit down.

The judge told him that if he did not sit down he should order his expulsion from the room, but counsel remained standing. He still insisted on his right to have an ex- ception noted, and the Court ordered the officer to remove him.

Do I understand that your honor has ordered me from the courtroom?' asked Mr. Coakley, and Judge Bond replied that he had so ordered. Meantime Court Offi- cer Campbell stepped beside Mr. Coakley and the latter accompanied him out of the room.

Mr Baker addressed the court as soon as Mr. Coakley had left. He told the judge that Mr. Coakley was familiar with the facts, and it was an injustice to the client that he should be excluded from the room. Counsel remarked that Mr. Coakley was rather enthusiastic in the interests of his client, but was not prompted by any per- sonal motive. He felt that the Court was wrong on this occasion, notwithstanding its wisdom and years of experience that the younger attorney had not attained.

He asked to have the order rescinded, and Judge Bond immediately revoked it, and Mr. Coakley came into the room. As the jury was filing out of the room at four o'clock, Mr. Coakley asked the Court to have the book used by the witness impound- ed by the clerk, as he wished to use it in cross-examination on Monday. He did not think the witness should be allowed to see it meantime. Judge Bond turned to Mr. Mellen, counsel for the defence, and said that Mr. Coakley was afraid to trust the records with counsel and asked if he had anything to say.

"I made no such statement. It is an en- tire misrepresentation," shouted Mr. Coak- ley, warmly, adding that he was willing that counsel should keep them, but did not want the witness to have them.

The Court asked Mr. Coakley then to state what he did want, and he replied that was just what he was there to state. "Well, then, state it," said the judge.

Mr. Coakley started in to explain certain discoveries he had made which prompted his making the request in regard to the books and the Court said he did not care to hear him talk.

Mr. Coakley said the only way he could tell the Court what he wanted was by the use of language. He then said he wanted an exception to what the Court had stated, and Judge Bond refused to allow it. Then he asked that it be noted that he excepted to the refusal to note the other exception.

His Honor would listen no longer to the attorney, and ordered the crier to adjourn court, which was done.

The case goes on Monday morning.

February 4, 1914

COAKLEY—In Brighton, Feb 4, Timothy W., beloved husband of Elizabeth J. Coakley (nee Smith). Funeral from 52 Parsons st Brighton, Saturday at 9 a m. Solemn high mass at St Columbkille's Church, Market st, at 10 a m.

"The College Beautiful"

"It is builded, our stately cloister, where Wisdom makes her home,

The stem-like columns flower into arch and sculptured dome,

The pillared halls are vaulted and lofty like the night

And each embrasured window is a rose of rainbow light.

Behold the court of science, and yonder the house of art;

And higher yet, God's altar, aflame with the Sacred Heart.

TIMOTHY WILFRED COAKLEY, '84.

NOTE: Boston College honored Coakley's poem celebrating the beauty of the college with this image that was used in several publications.

"LIFE IN DEATH"

by Edgar Allan Poe

NOTE: Edgar Allan Poe's short story "Life In Death" begins with an opium-smoking narrator who decides to risk eating a large piece of opium. The narrator tells the story of an eccentric artist who painted a picture of his wife but was so obsessed with painting the portrait that he paid no attention to his wife posing. When the artist finishes he finds that the painting is a life likeness, and "indeed Life itself." He turns to his bride and discovers she has died and her spirit was transferred into the lifelike painting, which is now flickering like a living flame. This was the inspiration for Coakley's story told by a kif-smoking narrator who paints a portrait of his spirit bride with terrifying consequences. The original story appeared in *Graham's Magazine,* April 1842 (pp. 200–201) in narrow columns as shown on the next pages. Poe made changes in subsequent printings including the title ("The Oval Portrait"), and deleted the first paragraph that explains the narrator's opium condition and his habit of smoking it with tobacco [weed] in a hookah. The illustration appeared with the revised story in 1895. The signature at the end was added for this RKS Library Edition. His usual signature was "E.A. Poe" with a simple paraph, if any, added to avoid forgery. Poe rarely signed his full name but in this full signature, dating to the time of the story, he added an elaborate paraph. Poe added an epigraph in Italian at the beginning of the story: "He and I live and speak if you did not observe the rule of silence." This inscription appeared beneath a painting of St. Bruno, who spent most of his life as a monk in solitude with a vow of silence. It was said that both the painting and his statue were so lifelike that they would speak if not for the vow. It is this life likeness that characterizes both *The Oval Portrait* and Abecassis' painting of Esther in Coakley's *Keef,* hence the story's alleged proof of life in death.

THE OVAL PORTRAIT

LIFE IN DEATH.

BY EDGAR A. POE.

Egli è vivo e parlerebbe se non osservasse la rigola del silentio.
Inscription beneath an Italian picture of St. Bruno.

My fever had been excessive and of long duration. All the remedies attainable in this wild Appennine region had been exhausted to no purpose. My valet and sole attendant in the lonely chateau, was too nervous and too grossly unskilful to venture upon letting blood—of which indeed I had already lost too much in the affray with the banditti. Neither could I safely permit him to leave me in search of assistance. At length I bethought me of a little pacquet of opium which lay with my tobacco in the hookah-case ; for at Constantinople I had acquired the habit of smoking the weed with the drug. Pedro handed me the case. I sought and found the narcotic. But when about to cut off a portion I felt the necessity of hesitation. In smoking it was a matter of little importance *how much* was employed. Usually, I had half filled the bowl of the hookah with opium and tobacco cut and mingled intimately, half and half. Sometimes when I had used the whole of this mixture I experienced no very peculiar effects; at other times I would not have smoked the pipe more than two-thirds out, when symptoms of mental derangement, which were even alarming, warned me to desist. But the effect proceeded with an easy gradation which deprived the indulgence of all danger. Here, however, the case was different. I had never *swallowed* opium before. Laudanum and morphine I had occasionally used, and about *them* should have had no reason to hesitate. But the solid drug I had never seen employed. Pedro knew no more respecting the proper quantity to be taken, than myself—and thus, in the sad emergency, I was left altogether to conjecture. Still I felt no especial uneasiness; for I resolved to proceed *by degrees*. I would take a *very* small dose in the first instance. Should this prove impotent, I would repeat it; and so on, until I should find an abatement of the fever, or obtain that sleep which was so pressingly requisite, and with which my reeling senses had not been blessed for now more than a week. No doubt it was this very reeling of my senses—it was the dull delirium which already oppressed me—that prevented me from perceiving the incoherence of my reason—which blinded me to the folly of defining any thing as either large or small where I had no preconceived standard of comparison. I had not, at the moment, the faintest idea that what I conceived to be an exceedingly small dose of solid opium might, in fact, be an excessively large one.

On the contrary I well remember that I judged confidently of the quantity to be taken by reference to the entire quantity of the lump in possession. The portion which, in conclusion, I swallowed, and swallowed without fear, was no doubt a very small proportion *of the piece which I held in my hand.*

The chateau into which Pedro had ventured to make forcible entrance rather than permit me, in my desperately wounded condition, to pass a night in the open air, was one of those fantastic piles of commingled gloom and grandeur which have so long frowned among the Appennines, not less in fact than in the fancy of Mrs. Radcliffe. To all appearance it had been temporarily and very lately abandoned. Day by day we expected the return of the family who tenanted it, when the misadventure which had befallen me would, no doubt, be received as sufficient apology for the intrusion. Meantime, that this intrusion might be taken in better part, we had established ourselves in one of the smallest and least sumptuously furnished apartments. It lay high in a remote turret of the building. Its decorations were rich, yet tattered and antique. Its walls were hung with tapestry and bedecked with manifold and multiform armorial trophies, together with an unusually great number of very spirited modern paintings in frames of rich golden arabesque. In these paintings, which depended from the walls not only in their main surfaces, but in very many nooks which the bizarre architecture of the chateau rendered necessary—in these paintings my incipient delirium, perhaps, had caused me to take deep interest ; so that having swallowed the opium, as before told, I bade Pedro to close the heavy shutters of the room—since it was already night—to light the tongues of a tall candelabrum which stood by the head of my bed—and to throw open far and wide the fringed curtains of black velvet which enveloped the bed itself. I wished all this done that I might resign myself, if not to sleep, at least alternately to the contemplation of these pictures, and the perusal of a small volume which had been found upon the pillow, and which purported to criticise and describe them.

Long—long I read—and devoutly, devotedly I gazed. I felt meantime, the voluptuous narcotic stealing its way to my brain. I felt that in its magical influence lay much of the gorgeous richness and variety of the frames—much of the ethereal hue that gleamed from the canvas—and much of the wild interest of the book which I perused. Yet this consciousness rather strengthened than impaired the delight of the illusion, while it weakened the illusion itself. Rapidly and gloriously the hours flew by, and the deep midnight came. The position of the candelabrum displeased me, and outreaching my hand with difficulty, rather than disturb my slumbering valet, I so placed it as to throw its rays more fully upon the book.

But the action produced an effect altogether unanticipated. The rays of the numerous candles (for there were many) now fell within a niche of the room which had hitherto been thrown into deep shade by one of the bed-posts. I thus saw in vivid light a picture all unnoticed before. It was the portrait of a young girl just ripened into womanhood. I glanced at the painting hurriedly, and then closed my eyes. Why I did this was not at first apparent even to my own perception. But while my lids remained thus shut, I ran over in mind my reason for so shutting them. It was an impulsive movement to gain time for thought—to make sure that my vision had not deceived me—to calm and subdue my fancy for a more sober and more certain gaze. In a very few moments I again looked fixedly at the painting.

That I now saw aright I could not and would not doubt ; for the first flashing of the candles upon that canvas had seemed to dissipate the dreamy stupor which was stealing over my senses, and to startle me into waking life as if with the shock of a galvanic battery.

The portrait, I have already said, was that of a young girl. It was a mere head and shoulders, done in what is technically termed a *vignette* manner ; much in the style of the favorite heads of Sully. The arms, the bosom and even the ends of the radiant hair, melted imperceptibly into the vague yet deep shadow which formed the back-ground of the whole. The frame was oval, richly, yet fantastically gilded and filagreed. As a work of art nothing could be more admirable than the painting itself. The loveliness of the face surpassed that of the fabulous Houri. But it could have been neither the execution of the work, nor the immortal beauty of the countenance, which had so suddenly and so vehemently moved me. Least of all, could it have been that my fancy, shaken from its half-slumber, had mistaken the head for that of a living person. I saw at once that the peculiarities of the design, of the *vignetting* and of the frame must have instantly dispelled such idea—must have prevented even its momentary entertainment. Thinking earnestly upon these points, I remained, for some hours perhaps,

half sitting, half reclining, with my vision riveted
upon the portrait. At length, satisfied of the true
secret of its effect, I fell back within the bed. I had
found the spell of the picture in a perfect *life-likeli-
ness* of expression, which at first startling, finally
confounded, subdued and appalled me. I could no
longer support the sad meaning smile of the half-
parted lips, nor the too real lustre of the wild eye.
With a deep and reverent awe I replaced the candelabrum in its former position. The cause of my deep
agitation being thus shut from view, I sought eagerly the volume which discussed the paintings and
their histories. Turning to the number which desig
nated the oval portrait, I there read the vague and
quaint words which follow :

"She was a maiden of rarest beauty, and not
more lovely than full of glee. And evil was the hour
when she saw, and loved, and wedded the painter.
He, passionate, studious, austere, and having already
a bride in his Art : she a maiden of rarest beauty
and not more lovely than full of glee : all light and
smiles and frolicksome as the young fawn : loving
and cherishing all things : hating only the Art which
was her rival : dreading only the pallet and brushes
and other untoward instruments which deprived her
of the countenance of her lover. It was thus a
terrible thing for this lady to hear the painter speak
of his desire to pourtray even his young bride. But
she was humble and obedient and sat meekly for
many weeks in the dark high turret-chamber where
the light dripped upon the pale canvas only from
overhead. But he, the painter, took glory in his
work, which went on from hour to hour and from
day to day. And he, was a passionate, and wild and

moody man, who became lost in reveries; so that he *would* not see that the light which fell so ghastily in that lone turret withered the health and the spirits of his bride, who pined visibly to all but him. Ye she smiled on and still on, uncomplainingly, because she saw that the painter, (who had high renown,) took a fervid and burning pleasure in his task, and wrought day and night to depict her who so loved him, yet who grew daily more dispirited and weak. And in sooth some who beheld the portrait spoke of its resemblance in low words, as of a mighty marvel and a proof not less of the power of the painter than of his deep love for her whom he depicted so surpassingly well. But at length, as the labor drew nearer to its conclusion, there were admitted none into the turret; for the painter had grown wild with the ardor of his work, and turned his visage from the canvas rarely, even to regard the countenance of his wife. And he *would* not see that the tints which he spread upon the canvas were drawn from the cheeks of her who sate beside him. And when many weeks had passed, and but little remained to do, save one brush upon the mouth and one tint upon the eye, the spirit of the lady again flickered up as the flame within the socket of the lamp. And then the brush was given, and then the tint was placed; and, for one moment, the painter stood entranced before the work which he had wrought; but in the next, while yet he gazed, he grew tremulous and very pallid, and aghast, and crying with a loud voice 'This is indeed *Life* itself!' turned himself suddenly round to his beloved—*who was dead*. The painter then added—' But is this indeed Death?' "

Edgar Allan Poe

HASHISH NEAR-DEATH EXPERIENCES
or
WHY KIF WILL BLOW YOUR HEAD OPEN
by
Ronald K. Siegel and Aida E. Hirschman *(dec.)*

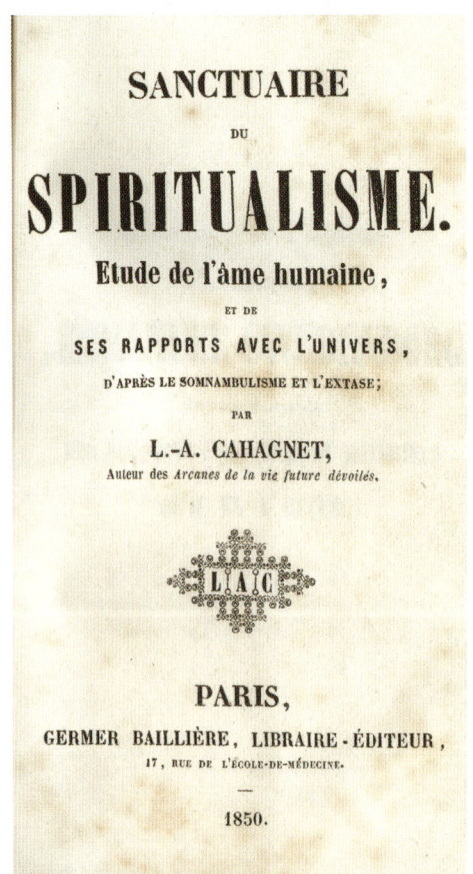

Hashish Near-Death Experiences

Ronald K. Siegel and Ada E. Hirschman
Department of Psychiatry and Biobehavioral Sciences
School of Medicine
University of California, Los Angeles

ABSTRACT

The historical literature on hashish-induced near-death experiences (NDEs) is reviewed, with particular reference to early French accounts. Most researchers endorsed the view of French psychiatrist Jacques Joseph Moreau that these experiences were hallucinations. Others, including spiritualist Louis-Alphonese Cahagnet, believed that hashish NDEs revealed an underlying reality as described in the works of Emanuel Swedenborg. Yet most accounts, resulting from high dosages, contained the elements and sequences of nondrug NDEs. Representative selections from this literature are translated here for the first time.

INTRODUCTION

Intoxication with hallucinogens has been associated with numerous subjective reports of death and dying. From the magical-religious uses of plant hallucinogens by New World Indians, through the psychedelic-assisted therapy of terminally ill cancer patients, to the recreational ecstasies of New Age users, the literature is replete with reports of hallucinations containing elements of near-death experiences (NDEs), if not afterlife voyages themselves (Harner, 1973; Kurland, Grof, Pahnke, and Goodman, 1973; Metzner, 1968). Perhaps more than any other hallucinogen, hashish has been associated with such NDEs. Early reports of hashish intoxications were so replete with these experiences that Aleister Crowley was prompted to comment in 1910 that "perhaps hashish is the drug which loosens the girders of the soul" (Regardie, 1968, p. 100). French spiritualist and psychopharmacologist Louis-Alphonese Cahagnet (1850) wrote that hashish allowed the soul to explore that spiritual world described by Emanuel Swedenborg (see Rhodes, 1982). Cahagnet collected his arguments and reports in a volume of hashish-induced NDEs (*The Sanctuary of Spiritualism*, 1850) and dedicated it to Swedenborg.

*Anabiosis — The Journal for Near-Death
Studies*, Spring 1984, Vol. 4, No. 1

Jules Giraud, a French hashish addict and writer, described one such experience in his 1913 *Testament d'un Haschischéen*:

> What? My turn to die? Not me! That would be too stupid! But a great blast of terror swept away my resistance and a frightful, measureless anguish possessed me. A glacial cold invaded my contracted legs and arms, and a blanket of ice crushed my chest. I drew a painful, oppressive breath, my ribs compressed into a corset like iron, and my breathing became more and more infrequent, even threatening to stop altogether [Giraud called to his medical companions for help, but they too had been stricken with an overdose of hashish] . . . . The path of the terrifying cold had finally reached my heart, which was no longer beating. From all available evidence I was going to die. . . . My implacable agony continued, but the appalling black void that had surrounded me up until then began to lighten a bit in a thundering downpour of insane, visionary images, such as happen to those about to drown. At the same time a splendid serenity before the fact of approaching death came over me bit by bit, making me forget my pain. . . . I was outside my body, spreading out in wonderful flashes of light, and I plunged my tentacles into the infinite, extending through all the past history of the Earth my mother, through all her geologic ages. . . . And among the glory of the stars, in an exploding apotheosis of suns and galaxies, I was the universal divinity. All this I saw from within. But from without it appears I was babbling, with furious gestures and hoarse, inarticulate cries. My acolytes, good hashish-fed medical men, were watching my crisis and wondering what to use for a straitjacket. In the end their presence and whispering pulled me down from my exaltation. . . . I repulsed them by incantations. . . . For I knew I was dead, for certain this time. And I finally knew Death's secret: by some means that I judged was habitual in dead people, what remained of my consciousness had become forever immobilized at the instant death seized me. But what a horrible, sinister idea—to embalm my soul within the illusion of this sepulchral chamber, behind whose windows there was nothing, I knew, nothing but the eternal void, absolute blackness, nonbeing (Kimmens, 1977, pp. 259-262).

These drug-induced experiences are generally viewed as hallucinations, and even Giraud reported that the above was a "macabre hallucination." While *elements* of NDEs have been reported for low-dose intoxications with hallucinogens like *Cannabis* (Siegel, 1980), there have been few accounts that have involved integrated sequences that more closely resemble the form, content, and qualitative aspects of the prototypical NDE (Ring, 1980). Such accounts may be associated with more toxic dosages that bring the subject closer to physical, and hence psychological, death. Giraud's experience occurred following ingestion of ten times the usual dose of hashish, prepared from the concentrated resins of the *Cannabis* plant. Using published historical recipes together with United Nations Narcotics

Commission assays of hashish used in the Middle East and France, we have calculated that the usual dose employed by nineteenth-century researchers represented 8.76-17.5 mg of delta-9-tetrahydro-cannabinol (THC, the active principle in *Cannabis*), but some groups, like the hashish club described below, used Giraud's dosage (87.6-175.2 mg of THC). These dosages differ substantially from contemporary social-recreational marijuana intoxications resulting from the smoking of a mixture of *Cannabis* leaves and stems delivering an average of 10 mg of THC. Consequently, the experiences are also different, as reported in early explorations of French and American researchers. This literature, having remained largely untranslated and forgotten, is reviewed here.

EARLY HISTORICAL DESCRIPTIONS

Originally an Old World plant that originated in the desert region in Central Asia, *Cannabis* was probably unknown in the Western hemisphere before the sixteenth century. Archeological specimens have been found in both Asia and Eastern Europe, indicating its use by man dates back more than 6,000 years. Coarse hemp fabrics excavated from some of the oldest sites of human habitation in Europe show that most, if not all, early uses were for fiber.

The ancient Chinese Emperor Shen-Nung (2737 B.C.) is credited with encouraging the first medicinal uses of *Cannabis*. From China the use of *Cannabis* spread to India, where its mind-altering properties were exploited (via drinking and smoking) in religious rituals. Among Muslim Indians, *Cannabis* was referred to as "joy-giver," "sky-flyer," "heavenly guide," "soother of grief," and "poor man's heaven." From India, use spread to the Middle East where the custom of eating hashish flourished.

Early Arabic manuscripts from the tenth to sixteenth centuries describe experiences wherein the hashish user died and was transported to another world (Rosenthal, 1971). While an overdose of potent hashish could result in real bodily death because of lowered blood pressure and body temperature (see Nahas, 1973; Walton, 1938), most "deaths" were psychological:

> By dissolving the moist elements in the body and thereby causing vapors [narcotic effects] to ascend to the brain, the hashish produces pernicious fancies, and by weakening the mind, it opens up the gate of fantasy (Rosenthal, 1971, p. 92).

An Arabic manuscript authored by al-Badrī (1464) notes that hashish users often see and hear a voice telling them that death approaches and the "secret" of the drug is that it permits "the spirit to ascend to the highest points in a heavenly ascension of disembodied understanding" (Rosenthal, 1971, p. 93). This ability of hashish to temporarily kill the physical body and liberate the spiritual was considered so potent that the murderous hashish eater was considered a suitable metaphor for the dangerous power of the drug. Accordingly, the poems and manuscripts of the period indicate that hashish makes every man a *hashishi* (assassin) unbeknown to himself. The contemporary myth of hashish-fortified assassins roaming throughout the Arabian nights represents little more than errors of translation and entymological misunderstanding. The assassin, a corruption of the word *hashishi*, was simply the hashish user who fell into a state of delirium wherein an ecstasy resembling an NDE could be experienced.

EARLY FRENCH EXPERIENCES

Hashish was introduced to Egypt in the thirteenth century and was widespread when Napoleon conquered that country in 1800. French physicians and psychiatrists followed Napoleon and returned to France with news of a hashish extract so potent that a user, as novelist Theophile Gautier wrote, could "taste the joys of Mohammed's heaven" (Ebin, 1961). Psychiatrist Jacques Joseph Moreau introduced hashish to his patients, colleagues, and friends. Among them was Gautier, who founded Le Club des Haschischins in 1841 and later described his experiences:

> The slightly convulsive gaiety of the beginning was succeeded by an undefinable sense of well-being, a calm without end. I was in the blessed phase of hashish. . . . No longer could I feel my body; the bonds between mind and matter were slender, I moved by simple desire into an environment which offered no resistance. . . . I dissolved into nothingness; I was freed from my ego, that odious and everpresent witness; for the first time I conceived the existence of elemental spirits—angels and souls separate from bodies (Ebin, 1961, pp. 11-12).

Moreau (1845) labeled these experiences hallucinations and went on to describe eight major elements of the hashish experience: general feelings of pleasure; increased excitement combined with a heightening of all senses; distortion of space and time; a keener sense of hearing combined with a greater susceptibility to music and the phenomenon that ordinary noise can be enjoyed as though it sounded sweet; persistent ideas; emotional disturbances; irresistible impulses; and illusions and hallucinations. Conspicuous among the hallucinations were experiences of dying and death. Gerard de Nerval, best friend of Gautier and member of Le Club, wrote in 1850 that "my soul was projected into past and future," whereby

> Hashish, in clouding the eyes of the body, enlightens those of the soul; the mind, once separated from the body, its weighty keeper, flies away like a prisoner whose jailer has fallen asleep with the key in the cell. It wanders happy and free in space and light, talking familiarly with the genii it meets, who astound with their sudden and delightful disclosures. It crosses in one easy bound through regions of indescribable happiness, all in the space of one minute that seems eternal (Kimmens, 1977, p. 108).

Contrary to Moreau's (1845) diagnosis of hallucination, de Nerval argued that these experiences were neither dreams nor hallucinations because "the hashish only brought forward a memory that had fled deep into my soul" (Kimmens, 1977, p. 109). Fellow Le Club member Charles Baudelaire (1851, 1860) also argued that the hashish experience, by its very involuntary nature, was reflecting, albeit with color and exaggeration, the very nature of a man's soul, and he likened the experience to Swedenborg's revelations of the spiritual state.

Other French writers contributed to descriptions of hashish experiences or else portrayed them in their own work. Physician Francois Lallemand was one of the first people in France to take hashish, and he submitted a thesis on the subject for the Doctor of Medicine degree in 1839. His book, *Le Hachych*, appeared in 1843, just as Le Club was being organized. A later edition appeared in 1848 with the cumbersome title *The 1848 Political and Social Revolution Predicted in 1843*, at which point Lallemand was a member of the Academy of Sciences and honorary professor at the University of Montpellier. Hashish provided Lallemand with a utopian vision of the future that was uncannily accurate in many detailed facts. For example, in one hashish experience he wrote:

> [I] arrived in America by way of California. I crossed the Rocky Mountains on a railway, then over the Great Lakes. I was present at the recognition of two new states, those of Wisconsin and Jowa [*sic*], which ceased being simple territories in order to become stars of the Union. I was one of the first to pass through the Panama Canal. Finally, after visiting the Cape of Good Hope, Timbuctu, and the Mountains of the Moon, I journeyed down the White Nile and saw the cataracts (Kimmens, 1977, p. 122).

The above passage was written during a hashish experience in 1843. The railroad did not cross the Rockies until 1869; Iowa joined the Union in 1846, Wisconsin in 1848; and the Panama Canal, not even begun until 1881, was finished in 1914. The Mountains of the Moon were not explored until the next century. These apparent "precognitive" and/or "prophetic" visions have been reported for other NDEs (Ring, 1982).

Other writers incorporated hashish experiences into works of fiction. For example, in Paris Alexander Dumas Père, while not a member of Le Club, wrote *Le Comte de Monte-Cristo* (1844), wherein he described how one of his characters reacted to hashish:

> His body seemed to acquire an immaterial lightness; his mind brightened in a remarkable manner; his senses seemed to double their powers. . . . An enchanting and mysterious harmony rose to God . . . as if some nymph . . . wanted to attract a soul there, or to build there a city. . . . Then amidst these immodest shades there glided, like a pure ray, like a Christian angel descending on Olympus, a chaste figure, a calm shadow, a soft vision, which seemed to veil its virgin brow against these marble impurities. . . . (Kimmens, 1977, pp. 137-138).

CAHAGNET'S HASHISH ECSTASIES

Independent of Moreau and Le Club activities, another group of French subjects, many of them followers of Swedenborg's philosophy, conducted experiments with hashish. They were led by Cahagnet. Cahagnet was born at Caen in 1805 and died at Argenteuil in 1885. He practiced a number of occupations including watchmaking and photography but was eventually attracted to spiritualism and the teachings of Swedenborg. Cahagnet authored 21 major occult and spiritual works, including the third major book (1850) ever written on hashish.

In an effort to explore the inner spiritual world, Cahagnet employed a variety of techniques including magnetism, electric shocks, burning incense, hemp seed, coriander, belladonna, anise, shellac, gum arabic, and even opium. But these methods failed to evoke the desired experience: "All I harvested was violent headaches. I don't know how I was able to withstand all these experiments" (Cahagnet, 1850, p. 101). Wandering about Paris, Cahagnet found a pharmacy selling hashish, purchased some, and began self-experimentation leading to numerous visions.

But Cahagnet denied that these visions were hallucinations. Rather, he argued that the hashish state revealed the spiritual state that one enters when one leaves the material state: the soul, liberated by hashish ("the medicine of the soul"), has the ability to observe and record universal truths. Just as Moreau (1845) argued that hashish allowed one to observe mental illness by provoking it artificially, Cahagnet interpreted that state ("the spiritual state as revealed by Swedenborg") as mental well-being and truth. And just as Moreau encouraged his students, colleagues, and fellow Le Club members to experiment with the drug, Cahagnet gave measured dosages to a number of colleagues and subjects. Furthermore, he had them record in minute detail a running commentary on their experiences, which he termed "ecstasies." He also debriefed them with a series of structured questions and gave them copies of Swedenborg's works to compare with their own experiences.

One of Cahagnet's subjects was identified as Mr. Lecocq, a marine clockmaker. His ecstasy is representative of the 14 others reported:

> I took three grams of hashish, and I soon recognized the effects of this limitless gaiety which results in dilating all the muscles, all the molecules of the body, and appear to leave the soul thus more detached from its envelope. I threw myself on a bed with perfect calm, having confidence in prayer, I addressed one to God and begged him to enlighten me, if he saw fit. At once I saw myself gradually raised up passing by different luminous colors. . . . What pure light! What a feeling! That happiness! That rapture! . . . Following I saw, in a distance that seemed limitless to me, a luminous circle the same in color and light as that previously observed, and from the center of this creative hearth escaped bundles composed of luminous points of all colors. . . . Upon seeing this continual creation of luminous points which ended up spreading into a grandiose space, it seemed to me that I became smaller at the same time I was raising myself to admire what I saw. . . . I noticed that I was not actually in my body. . . . I entered one of those beautiful ecstasies where the soul seems to leave the earth, ascend to the celestial regions, and finds itself thus enveloped in a light that penetrates to the point of producing the most agreeable and profound feeling that could exist. Oh! I admit I was in a rapture impossible to describe. How grandiose in scope creation appeared! Oh! Yes, I was overcome before this infinite grandeur of God, not painfully overcome, but rather by a feeling of joy and admiration. . . . Those are the principal scenes which I saw in this hashish seance, which confirmed my first experience, leaving me with the conviction that all these images are not the fruit of hallucination, if by this word one understands illusion, or misunderstanding. Not knowing yourself what will appear to you, how can you say you create what you see, if that were so, the wonder could not take place, all the sensations of the soul would be entirely worthless, and you would be able to alter them, which does not happen (Cahagnet, 1850, pp. 196-200).

Selections from the remaining hashish ecstasies containing elements similar to those found in NDEs are provided below. They are grouped according to the major categories discussed by Ring (1980) and Moody (1975):

Peace and the Sense of Well-Being

> "Calm followed" (p. 134).

> "What happiness! . . . What ecstasy!" (p. 139).

> "I am happier than a king" (p. 179).

> "I only know that I was perfectly happy" (p. 194).

Body Separation

> "Detached from my material body as I felt I was" (p. 106).

> "I saw myself dying; my body was lying on a bed, and my soul was escaping from all parts of it like a thick, black smoke; but instead of dissipating in the atmosphere, this smoke condensed two feet above my body and formed a body exactly like the one it had just left. Oh! How beautiful it is, I exclaimed. Alphonse, my friend, I have just died. I understand death. I understand how one dies, and why one dies. Oh! How sublime it is. Then I went into a state of which I have no memory at all" (p. 121).

> "My material body evaporates, my voice is no longer mine: I am no longer myself!" (p. 139).

Entering the Darkness

> "Then my apprehension increased to a degree that I cannot express" (p. 121).

> "A state of darkness which one could truly call the lobby of life" (p. 178).

> "The color black appeared to me to come out of the handsome hall resplendent in its clarity" (p. 197).

Seeing the Light

> "It is a white mist like milk, it is an even white light" (p. 140).

> "It is like a white light, pure and alone" (p. 141).

> "What light I see" (p. 155).

"I see little luminous globes that rise up to the infinite heights; I am told that these are the souls rising to heaven" (p. 156).

"The light left this immensity which I was leaving as if from a little hole, enlarging into a sort of funnel, dividing into rays like golden wires" (p. 170).

"They are as brilliant as the sun" (p. 182).

"It seemed to me that this hall of light, this center of universal attraction was God" (p. 193).

Entering the Light

"This phenomenon is remarkable and gave me awareness of a very deep gratification of the passage of our terrestrial state to the spiritual state which we call death. I felt all the pains of the last moments of our material existence. I passed through agony and through death; this last moment of our life which brings so many tears to our dear ones, and which each one dreads as being the most painful, is on the contrary the one where the soul enters the vast land of liberty, the one where one breathes at one's ease and rejoices in the most pleasant sensations that one can imagine; it is the moment of supreme happiness" (pp. 183-184).

Ineffability

"I find it impossible to describe" (p. 107).

"I would give five hundred thousand francs if . . . you could see what I see" (p. 122).

"What I feel, what I experience at this moment, it is impossible for you to understand. Here, friend, listen, I will try to explain it to you. But in fact no, it is useless, because I know that you would not understand" (p. 124).

"I cannot write all that I said and especially all that I saw during those three hours, words cannot express the feelings that the soul experiences" (p. 134).

"I was in a rapture impossible to describe" (p. 199).

Perceived Reality

"There are no hallucinations, there are only disordered observations" (p. 111).

"Eh! Don't object that I was in a sort of hallucination which made it impossible for me to judge soundly; for I declare, never was my spirit so calm, never did I rejoice in a greater fullness of my reason" (p. 177).

"I looked on it as reality and not as a dream. A dream is only in this world; truth, light are in the other. They appear to you as soon as one penetrates it momentarily and even by an artificial means" (p. 181).

"Death is a state of the soul, another manner in which it can see things. I have died fifty times, by passing through fifty different states, in which I can observe different degrees of creation. . . . I leave it to the reader to judge whether in our material state we can raise ourselves to this height of conception and if these solutions feel like hallucination?" (pp. 202, 204).

Life Review

"The most beautiful sight a man could see was the reward for my sufferings, a vast panorama, where all that I would have seen, thought or known in my life was portrayed in brilliant colors, in the form of transparent pictures like window shades, lit from behind with an unequaled light. This panorama unrolled around me, turning with great brightness" (p. 108).

Encounters with Others

"A little ways away I see two spirits meet, to begin with they are much more beautiful, the woman, has long hair, she looks like Eve, as she is generally portrayed" (p. 127).

"At that moment I seemed to see the creator in a great light with the appearance of the human form" (p. 136).

"He sensed that his brother [dead] was there before him" (p. 151).

"I saw souls by the thousands. What was most surprising to me, was that I knew that they were souls and they did not have human forms, rather they were little spheres or balls barely as big as the end of a little finger, they were of a dazzling whiteness" (pp. 169-170).

"I looked at . . . my little girl, my Stephanie, who died at the age of nine. The face of this beloved child . . . appeared . . . in the clearest manner, the most striking, the most minutely exact. Even more, I saw her holding the index finger of her right hand in her nose; a habit she had developed in the last days of her lingering death, and of which I had no recall. At the end of an indefinite time, but nevertheless long enough so that I had no doubt of the reality of the vision, her face faded as it had appeared . . ." (p. 191).

Auditory Sensations

"What harmony! What subtle music! How grand it all is, how sublime!" (pp. 157-158).

"Each of his nerves and fibers seemed to him to be a harmonious chord which corresponds to these same instruments and gives a sound which, mingled with a great number of others . . . leaves his senses with a musical impression as complicated as it was aggreeable" (pp. 160-161).

Visions or Thoughts of Great Knowledge

"God is so good that he has permitted me who knows nothing, to understand the marvels of the creation" (p. 122).

"Swedenborg was right to say that we have a universe in us, because I can embrace the whole universe at one time" (p. 124).

"Swedenborg, whom we revere so, was not in a different state than I; I see what he saw, I understand what he understood" (p. 126).

"I understand eternity" (p. 126).

"I also understood what space and creation was" (p. 136).

"It is heaven that I see, allow me, send me, oh my God, to men to tell and explain your law. . . . Men dwell in such ignorance; I was ignorant as they are, but if they knew what I know now!" (pp. 155-156).

"Now I must tell you how I thought I understood God" (p. 192).

Altered Sense of Time and Space

"I felt it [my body] stretch out into infinity" (p. 143).

"One cannot express the speed with which this multitude of pictures passes before the eyes of the spirit" (p. 182).

"The rapid succession in which the scenes that I saw took place proved to me that I could see in one second that which would take me years to observe in my material state; therefore there is no time in that state" (p. 183).

Threshold and Return

"I was no longer on earth, I would have liked never to return, but I thought of my family, and I understood that I had to return" (p. 135).

"I enjoyed myself enormously in this state of light, and as I was completely aware that it was not clear to me, I felt myself seized with regret at the thought that I would have to abandon it in a few moments to return to the material life, a regret that was not sweetened by the knowledge that I would return one day" (p. 178).

"Here ends the interesting and enlightening portion of my experiment. After that moment, it appeared that I entered a rather bizarre state. . . . I have very faint memory of this state. . . . A few cold breaths on the head and several swallows of vinegar-water, which you made me swallow, and sponging of the forehead and temples with the same water halted the attack and I reentered ordinary life" (p. 194).

Aftereffects

"Everything seemed sad to me compared to that which I had seen. The feelings of the soul are so vivid, and if one feels again such great happiness, all the earthly emotions and joys seem as nothing; but everything went away and although always having the memory of these pictures, one enters into the earthly state with too much regret" (p. 138).

"Under the influence of hashish one is absolutely convinced of this profound truth, and although rid of this influence it remains in your spirit for life" (pp. 200-201).

EARLY AMERICAN EXPERIENCES

While Moreau, Le Club, and Cahagnet were exploring hashish-induced experiences in France, independent experimentation was reported by several Americans traveling in Egypt and Syria. Bayard Taylor (1855) described his experiences in one of the earliest accounts by an American. Taylor found that hashish helped

to divest my frame of its earthly and material nature, until my substance appeared to me no grosser than the vapors of the atmosphere. . . . The sense of limitation—of the confinement of our senses within the bounds of our flesh and blood—instantly fell away. The walls of my frame were burst outward and tumbled into ruin; and, without thinking what form I wore—losing sight even of all idea of form—I felt that I existed throughout a vast extent of space. . . . It is difficult to describe this sensation. . . . The physical feeling of extended being was accompanied by the image of an exploding meteor. . . . Every effort to preserve my reason was accompanied by a pang of mortal fear. . . . The thought of death, which also haunted me, was far less bitter than this dread. I knew that in the struggle which was going on in my frame, I was borne fearfully near the dark gulf. . . . My companion was now approaching the same condition. . . . He cried out to me that he was dying . . . but what is death to madness? (pp. 134-146).

Taylor's experience included visions of unusual lights, music, and wondrous constructions of jewels and stone. These constructions were also described by an anonymous lawyer who resided in Damascus for five years and became an habitué of hashish. In the September

1856 issue of *Putnam's Magazine* he wrote:

> I stood in divine elevation above a marble altar. There were giant colonnades
> on either side, sweeping forward to a monstrous portal, through which
> I beheld countless sphinxes facing each other down an interminable
> avenue of granite. Before me, in the mighty space between the columns,
> was a multitude of men, all bowing with their faces to the earth, while
> priests chanted anthems to my praise as the great Osiris. But suddenly,
> before I could shake the temple with my nod, I saw one in the image of
> Christ enter the portal and advance through the crowd to the foot of my
> altar. It was not Christ the risen and glorified; but the human and crucified
> Jesus of Nazareth. I knew him by his grave sweetness of countenance. . . .
> He beckoned me to descend. . . . He disappeared, and when I rose the
> temple had disappeared also. . . . (Ebin, 1961, p. 60).

The over-the-counter availability of patent medicine extracts of
Cannabis provided others in nineteenth-century America easy
access to the experience. The first full-length English work to appear
on hashish was *The Hasheesh Eater* by FitzHugh Ludlow (1857),
published anonymously while he was a student at Union College in
Schnectady, New York.

Typically, Ludlow (1857) reported his hashish experiences as
hallucinations wherein:

> The moment that I closed my eyes a vision of celestial glory burst upon
> me. I stood on the silver strand of a translucent, boundless lake, across
> whose bosom I seemed to have been just transported. A short way up the
> beach, a temple, modeled like the Parthenon, lifted its spotless and gleaming
> columns of alabaster sublimely into a rosy air—like the Parthenon, yet as
> much excelling it as the godlike ideal of architecture must transcend that
> ideal realized by man. Unblemished in its purity of whiteness, faultless in
> the unbroken symmetry of every line and angle, its pediment was draped
> in odorous clouds, whose tints outshone the rainbow. It was the work of
> an unearthly builder, and my soul stood before it in a trance of ecstasy. . . .
> I pass in. . . . An atmosphere of fathomless and soul-satisfying serenity
> surrounded and transfused me. . . . They were all clad in flowing robes,
> like God's highpriests, and each one held in his hand a lyre of unearthly
> workmanship. . . . While his celestial chords were trembling up into their
> sublime fullness, another strikes his strings, and now they blend upon my
> ravished ear in such a symphony as was never heard elsewhere, and I shall
> never hear again out of the Great Presence. . . . Throughout all the infini-
> tudes around me I looked out, and met no boundaries of space. . . .
> With ecstasy the whole soul drank in revelations from every province,
> and cried out, "Oh, awful loveliness!" . . . Through whatever region or
> circumstance I passed, one characteristic of the vision remained unchanged:
> peace—everywhere godlike peace, the sum of all conceivable desires
> satisfied (pp. 34-42).

But on at least one occasion he took an excessive dosage resulting in a particularly traumatic experience:

> In the course of my delirium, the soul, I plainly discovered, had indeed departed from the body. I was that soul utterly divorced from the corporeal nature, disjoined, clarified, purified. From the air in which I hovered I looked down upon my former receptical. . . . This was neither hallucination nor dream. The sight of my reason was preternaturally intense, and I remembered that this was one of the states which frequently occur to men immediately before their death has become apparent to lookers-on, and also in the more remarkable conditions of trance. That such a state is possible is incontestably proved by many cases on record in which it has fallen under the observation of students most eminent in physico-psychical science. A voice of command called on me to return into the body, saying in the midst of my exultation over what I thought was my final disenfranchisement from the corporeal, "The time is not yet." I returned, and again felt the animal nature joined to me by its mysterious threads of conduction. Once more soul and body were one (pp. 74-75).

In an experience vaguely reminiscent of Giraud's medically supervised hashish experiment, American novelist Mary Hungerford described in 1884 her "overdose" of hashish:

> The physicians asked then the size and time of the last dose, but I could not answer. . . . In the midst of it all I left my body, and quietly from the foot of the bed watched my unhappy self nodding with frightful velocity. I glanced indignantly at the shamefully indifferent group that did not even appear to notice the frantic motions, and resumed my place in my living temple of flesh in time to recover sufficiently to observe one doctor lift his finger from my wrist, where he had laid it to count the pulsations just as I lapsed into unconsciousness, and say to the other: "I think she moved her head. She means us to understand that she has taken largely of the cannabis indica." . . . I died, as I believed, although by a strange double consciousness I knew that I should again reanimate the body I had left. In leaving it I did not soar away, as one delights to think of the freed spirits soaring. Neither did I linger around dear, familiar scenes. I sank, an intangible, impalpable shape, through the bed, the floors, the the cellar, the earth, down, down, down! (Palmer and Horowitz, 1982, pp. 88-89).

Believing she was dead, Hungerford became possessed by fear and loneliness:

> It was not only death I feared with a wild, unreasoning terror, but there was a fearful expectation of judgment, which must, I think, be like the torture of lost souls. . . . In place of my lost senses I had a marvelously keen sixth sense of power, which I can only describe as an intense super-

human consciousness that in some way embraced all the fine and went immeasurably beyond. . . . As time went on, and my dropping through space continued, I became filled with the most profound loneliness (Walton, 1938, pp. 97-98).

Chemist Victor Robinson (1912), following in the footsteps of Moreau (1845) and Cahagnet (1850), conducted a series of experiments and careful observations of hashish. He described a typical experience:

> I hear music. . . . The magic of that melody bewitches my soul. I begin to rise horizontally from my couch. No walls impede my progress, and I float into the outside air. Sweeter and sweeter grows the music, it bears me higher and higher, and I float in tune with the infinite—under the turquoise heavens where globules of mercury are glittering. . . . I am transported to wonderland. I walk in streets where gold is dirt. . . . Some faces are strange, some I knew on earth, but all are lovely. They smile, and sing and dance. . . . I hear my sister come home from the opera. I wish to call her. . . . The result is a fizzle. No sound issues from my lips. My lips do not move. I give it up. . . . Then the vision grows so wondrous, that body and soul I give myself up to it, and I taste the fabled joys of paradise. Ah, what this night is worth! (pp. 66-71)

Despite the vividness, spontaneity, and involuntariness of these images, Robinson, like many other American hashish users, recognized them as hallucinations: "I know they are not real, I know I see them because I took hasheesh, but they annoy me nevertheless" (Robinson, 1912, p. 72).

COMMENTS

The annoyance expressed by Robinson has been echoed throughout the French and American hashish literature. While the majority of writers endorsed the interpretation first suggested by Moreau (1845) that these hashish-induced NDEs were simply hallucinations, others, like Cahagnet (1850) and his group of Swedenborg followers, believed in an underlying spiritual reality. Cahagnet's ecstasies clearly described the major elements and sequences of NDEs, although it should be noted that they were not present in every intoxication. Indeed, at least one subject failed to report any subjective experience. But many of his subjects had visions, if not beliefs as well, of dying, death, and an afterlife. While their Swedenborg-inspired spiritual set and setting, important determinants of hallucinogenic experiences, undoubtedly influenced their NDEs, such "spiritual"-

flavored experiences also appeared, albeit less dramatically, among reports from other French and American users. Yet all mentioned common NDE elements and sequences.

Taken together, this literature suggests that hashish-induced experiences lie on a continuum ranging from mild inebriation to stages of dissociation, out-of-body experiences, hallucinations, and NDEs. The stages are not clearly divisible and any given stage may contain elements of the others, thus illustrating an inherent difference in the dynamics of hashish and nonhashish NDEs. The experience of moving along this continuum appears to be marked by changes in perceived reality. With low dosages of hashish, users view events as separate from themselves (e.g., seeing a light). Higher dosages produce a sensation of involvement in the events (e.g., going into the light). Concomitantly, images initially perceived as being "like" or "similar" to real events are perceived, with high dosages, as being "in fact" real events. Thus, the differences between the hashish NDEs and other nondrug NDEs appears to be more a function of dosage or intensity than the fact that a drug was or was not used to trigger the experience.

The high dosages of THC employed by Cahagnet and others invite speculation regarding an actual toxic threat to the body, perhaps common to the hashish NDE. While few subjects have actually died from hashish poisoning, we are unlikely to know for certain just how life-threatening these hashish intoxications are. Contemporary research guidelines prevent human subjects from receiving dosages equivalent (up to 175 mg THC) to those discussed here. Theoretically, these dosages are in the range of those expected to be lethal in approximately four percent of the intoxications (Nahas, 1973). Death would result from coma and respiratory arrest. But even in intoxications with lower dosages of 10-20 mg THC (Siegel and Jarvik, 1975), similar NDE elements can be found. To the extent that an overdose of hashish produces death, higher doses should produce more intense NDEs, and that is exactly what happens. Whether or not this reflects incipient death is unknown. But the resultant high-dose experience is more similar to a classical NDE than a traditional hashish intoxication or hallucination.

The hashish-induced NDE, as examined in the work of Cahagnet (1850) and others, is more strikingly similar to nondrug-induced experiences than was previously noted in a discussion of drug-induced NDEs (Siegel, 1980). While such similarity cannot resolve questions concerning the reality of a hashish-induced NDE, Moreau's (1845) explanation as hallucination was rejected by those who experienced it. Indeed, Cahagnet, having read Moreau's book, commented that Moreau was only "struggling with the need to find new terms to classify the different states of the soul which are contained in dreams, thoughts, hallucinations, or derangement. . . . Suffice it to say that he is neither against us nor with us" (Cahagnet, 1850, p. 283). In keeping with this spirit, the present review of hashish-induced experiences adds to the catalog of situations associated with NDEs; it does not argue their interpretation.

REFERENCES

Baudelaire, C. Du vin et du hachisch comparés comme moyens de multiplication de l'individualité. *Le Messages de L'Assemblee*, March, 1851.

Baudelaire, C. *Les Paradis Artificiels. Opium et Haschisch.* Paris: Poulet-Malassis et de Broise, 1860.

Cahagnet, L. A. *Sanctuaire du Spiritualism.* Paris: Germer Baillière, 1850.

Ebin, D. (Ed.). *The Drug Experiences.* New York: Orion Press, 1961.

Harner, M. J. (Ed.). *Hallucinogens and Shamanism.* New York: Oxford University Press, 1973.

Kimmens, A. C. (Ed.). *Tales of Hashish.* New York: William Morrow, 1977.

Kurland, A. A., Grof, S., Pahnke, W. N., and Goodman, L. E. Psychedelic drug assisted psychotherapy with terminal cancer. In I. K. Goldberg, S. Malitz, and A. H. Kutscher (Eds.), *Psychopharmacologic Agents for the Terminally Ill & Bereaved.* New York: Foundation of Thanatology/Columbia University Press, 1973.

Ludlow, F. *The Hasheesh Eater.* New York: Harper & Brothers, 1857.

Metzner, R. (Ed.). *The Ecstatic Adventure.* New York: Macmillan, 1968.

Moody, R. A. *Life After Life.* Covington, GA: Mockingbird, 1975.

Moreau, J. *Du Hachisch et de L'Alienation Mentale.* Paris: Librairie de Fortin, 1845.

Nahas, G. G. *Marihuana—Deceptive Weed.* New York: Raven Press, 1973.

Palmer, C., and Horowitz, M. (Eds.). *Shaman Woman, Mainline Lady.* New York: William Morrow, 1982.

Regardie, I. *Roll Away the Stone*. Saint Paul: Llewellyn Publications, 1968.

Rhodes, L. S. The NDE enlarged by Swedenborg's vision. *Anabiosis*, 1982, *2*(1), 15-35.

Ring, K. *Life at Death*. New York: Coward, McCann and Geoghegan, 1980.

Ring, K. Precognitive and prophetic visions in near-death experiences. *Anabiosis*, 1982, *2*(1), 47-74.

Robinson, V. *An Essay on Hasheesh*. New York: Medical Review of Reviews, 1912.

Rosenthal, F. *The Herb. Hashish versus Medieval Muslim Society*. Leiden, The Netherlands: E. J. Brill, 1971.

Siegel, R. K. The psychology of life after death. *American Psychologist*, 1980, *35*(10), 911-931.

Siegel, R. K., and Jarvik, M. E. Drug-induced hallucinations in animals and man. In R. K. Siegel and L. J. West (Eds.), *Hallucinations: Behavior, Experience, and Theory*. New York: Wiley, 1975.

Taylor, B. *The Land of the Saracen; or, Pictures of Palestine, Asia Minor, Sicily, and Spain*. New York: G. P. Putnam, 1855.

Walton, R. P. *Marihuana. America's New Drug Problem*. Philadelphia: J. B. Lippincott, 1938.

AFTERWORD
KIF (or Keef) AND DEATH

Pulitzer Prize playwright Tennessee Williams noticed "hallucinatory visitations" or unbidden memories of friends that indicated part of him was dying in February 1983. Death-dreams became enhanced thanks due to the sedative Secobarbital covered-up by alcohol. He retreated to the drugs, especially chain-smoking kif with either chilled vodka or white vermouth. He had frequently travelled to Tangier to visit Paul Bowles, a local writer/sorcerer who found magical properties in drugs, sex and music. Williams and other writers felt they could speak with Bowles through the words and pictures of memoirs, even speak to him beyond the grave. Bowles liked hot *majoun*, a paste made of hashish served with glasses of mint tea, and the relaxing smells of kif burning with tobacco in the pipe and *shaqfa*, the clay bowl. Williams died on February 25, 1983. Prior to that he enjoyed a last visit to his home in Key West, Florida where writer Jane Bowles' summer house was on his property.

Tennessee Williams, born Thomas Lanier Williams III (1911-1983). He smoked Cannabis including marijuana at the *Café de Paris* in Tangiers where kif was a limitless drug of choice. Later in life, Williams mixed smoke with deadly drug habits: amphetamines, Seconal, alcohol, and injections of prescribed medications. Williams' friend Dotson Rader chronicled this expansive drug use in his memoir *Cry of the Heart* and more recently in the new play *God Looked Away*.

My own scout Jane tried sniffing mint leaves in the Moroccan Desert. Despite a healthy physical appearance she handled everything with a careful well-traveled method. She stayed away from the kif and brandy that gave Jane Bowles a stroke and spasms at age 40 affecting her sight and capacity to imagine. She continued to write but her health declined due to chronic kif smoking, alcoholism, and recreational use of "magic" medicines. My Jane, now a healthy runner and agility trainer, returned to California with pictures and a colorful rug for the RKS Library of Drug Literature.

Paul Bowles, a Tangier storyteller in his apartment preparing tea and a local drug called *majoun*. He smoked kif, a mixture of Cannabis and tobacco, but didn't inhale. *Majoun* was eaten as Cannabis "jam" made with honey, nuts, figs, dates and kif.

Most of Paul Bowles' stories assumed the aspect of magic banishing the existent world while creating a new world that is more inhabitable. He often spoke about death as in the final pages of his autobiography *Without Stopping*:

> The Moroccans claim that full participation in life demands the regular contemplation of death. I agree without reserve. Unfortunately I am unable to conceive of my own death without setting it in the far more terrible mise en scène of old age. There I am without teeth, unable to move, wholly dependent upon someone who I pay to take care of me and who at any moment may go out of the room and never return. Of course this is not at all what the Moroccans mean by the contempla-

tion of death; they would consider my imaginings a particularly contemptible form of fear. One culture's therapy is another culture's torture. "Good-by," says the dying man to the mirror they hold in front of him. "We won't be seeing each other any more." When I quoted Valéry's epigram in *The Sheltering Sky*, it seemed a poignant bit of fantasy. Now because I no longer imagine myself as an onlooker at the scene, but instead as the principle protagonist, it strikes me as repugnant. To make it right, the dying man would have to add two words to his little farewell and they are: "**Thank God!**" [1]

Why "Thank God"? Paul Bowles answers[2]:

> I'm not interested in immortality. A lot of people are, I know. That's what most religions are about. But all religions are absurd. Immortality is one sliver of their absurdity. They all seem to like the idea of living beyond death. I wonder why . . . Oh, I'm willing to admit that it's possible that people might remember me for some years after I die.

"These borders between the dead and the living are not hermetically sealed."   —W.G. Sebald[3]

Always the writer or "writerally" Paul told his biographer that "the death of the main character does not make the book satisfactory. The book has to go on." *Majoun* revived his memory. He headed for the desert and madness. It was the only way of making it satisfactory and appropriating fictionalization. Paul Bowles described his experience with *majoun* while on a rock high on a hillside above his cottage:

> The effect came upon me suddenly, and I lay absolutely still, feeling myself being lifted, rising to meet the sun. For a long time I did not open my eyes. Then I felt that I had risen so far about the rock that I was afraid to open them. In another

---

1 Quotation from *Paul Bowles, Magic & Morocco* by Allen Hibbard. San Francisco: Cadmus Editions, 2004, pp. 158–159.

2 Paul Bowles, interview with Phillip Ramey, December 1997.

3 Born Winfried George Sebald in 1944; known as great German academic and writer; died in 2001 at 57 years old in a car crash. He wrote novels, poetry, and achieved book awards in the United States for a Holocaust German novel *Austerlitz*. Munich: C. Hanser, 2001, translated by Anthea Bell.

hour my mind was behaving in a fashion I should never have imagined possible. I wanted to get off the boulders, down the mountainside, and back home as fast as I could. When I returned to the Farhar, the sun was low. I could see its pink light fading on the villa that edged the cliffs across the valley. There were cypresses outside the cottage; they stood unprotected, high above the sea, directly in the blast if the *cherqi*, which roared through them with a sound louder than that of the waves against the rocks. . . . Later that night I noted a good many details, and the next day wrote out much of the scene. . . . It is certain that the *majoun* provided a solution totally unlike whatever I should have found without it.[4]

Although Paul Bowles smoked kif for many years, it became a regular habit in search of "a way out of the phenomenological world." He believed in the kif world and in the 1960s he wrote the short stories in *A Hundred Camels in the Courtyard*[5] with the idea that the drug opened new doors of perception just like LSD worked for the psychedelic explorer Timothy Leary during the same period, mapping the new world of consciousness as a passageway to enlightment in the "other" physical world. In fact, according to Bowles himself, having been unable to make literary use of several "incidents and situations," he smoked kif as a tool to conjure up the narrative for these four stories. "Thus, for a dedicated smoker, the passage to the 'other world' is often a pilgrimage undertaken for the express purpose of oracular consultation... I was able to use Cannabis both as solvent and solder in the construction."[6]

Bowles acquired more *majoun* and became better acquainted with its properties and the ideal conditions under which to ingest it. It allowed him to visualize events but it wasn't a substitute for the real experience. He could revive his memory of the real events and thereby produce what Bowles called "a novel from memory."

---

4 Christopher Sawyer-Laucanno. *An Invisible Spectator. A Biography of Paul Bowles.* New York: Weidenfeld & Nicolson, 1989. Quotation, p. 265.

5 Bowles, Paul. *A Hundred Camels in the Courtyard.* San Francisco: City Lights Books, 1962. [Priced at $1.25]

6 Liner notes from recording of *Paul Bowles Reads A Hundred Camels in the Courtyard*, A Cadmus Editions/Dom America Audio Book, 1973.

His readers roaming through the American expatriate community in Tangier allowed Bowles to become the spiritual father of the Beat movement. Besides Williams they all signed on for the trip:

"As a short-story writer, Bowles has had few equals in the second half of the twentieth century."

—Gore Vidal

"Paul Bowles opened the world of Hip. He let in the murder, the drugs, the incest, the death of the Square...the call of the orgy, the end of civilization."

—Norman Mailer

"His work is art. At his best, Bowles has no peer."

—*Time*

"I think one is always writing about oneself. But you are writing about transformations of experience. In good writing, the works come out as something very different from the experience itself...Writing is, I suppose, a superstitious way of keeping horror at bay, of keeping evil outside."

—Paul Bowles

A clever Jane discovered smelling mint leaves suppressed the strong odor inside a leather tannery that she was visiting without resorting to hot *majoun* and glasses of mint tea.

Paul Bowles' first novel *The Sheltering Sky* (1949) was an immediate best-seller and the *New York Times* compared the author to Camus, Sartre, and Genet. He became a literary star with intimates such as Truman Capote, Gertrude Stein, Aaron Copland, Allen Ginsberg, William Burroughs, among others. He traveled throughout the world winning accolades and admirers in music and literature. But then he went into voluntary exile in Morocco and later in the remoteness of Africa. Not surprising, both Bowles and his works were surrounded by mystique and remained with that tattoo wherever they went, destined to continue forever.

Paul had spent a year earlier in the Sahara hearing stories that urged him to write fictional versions. He wanted to use them in his story "The Delicate Prey," full of macabre and horror tales:

> Three Moslem merchants had been murdered on their way across the desert. The killer had appropriated their caravan and gone on with it....They reported their suspicions to the military authorities who gave them carte blanche....Accordingly they carried the man far out in the desert and buried him up to his neck in the sand; then they left him to die.

Bowles, like T.W. Coakley, became a follower of horror writer Edgar Allan Poe. Tennessee Williams and other admirers found such stories hard to take but some felt the powerful terrifying ability of Bowles' writing. He provided detailed descriptions of such things as torture and violence that can produce ugly scenes. Bowles achieved what Alexandro Jodorowsky[7] did in the 1971 film *El Topo:* Show and tell about a violent torture scene like castration. Consider the following excerpts from Bowles' *Collected Stories:*

> The man moved and surveyed the young body lying on the stones. He ran his finger along the razor's blade: a pleasant excitement took possession of him. He stepped over, looked down, and saw the sex that sprouted from the base of the belly. Not entirely conscious of what he was doing, he took it in one hand and brought his other arm down with the motion of a reaper wielding a sickle. It was swiftly severed. A round dark hole

---

7 Jodorowsky, Alexandro. *El Topo*. A book of the film scene-by-scene narrative by Jodorowsky who was director, star, writer and composer. Douglas Book: World Publishing Company, 1971. Translations by Joanne Pottlitzer.

was left, flush with the skin; he stared a moment, blankly. Driss was screaming. The muscles all over his body stood out, moved.

Slowly the Moungari (hunter) smiled, showing his teeth. He put his hand on the hard belly and smoothed the skin. Then he made a small vertical incision there, and using both hands, studiously stuffed the loose organ in until it disappeared.

The story is like a near-death-dream with the dreamer under the influence of kif or other potent Cannabis smoke with nightmarish visions as depicted on page 179.

Weeks later I found a handwritten letter that slipped from inside my copy of *An Invisible Spectator* from biographer Christopher

Paul Bowles (1910–1999) Smoking Kif.

Sawyer-Laucanno, who was delighted to get readers equally delighted in his portrait of Paul Bowles' work. I accepted the coincidence and attributed it to the magic of Morocco. After all, the envelope featured an American flag with a 1989 Yosemite stamp still in good shape. It told me that Paul finally came home to one of the most beautiful natural parks in America.

Bowles continued to write *The Sheltering Sky*, describing it as "a novel just like any other novel." Reluctantly he found that the sexual adventures of his writing failed to provide relief with his wife Jane. This theme of frustrated sexuality and failed attempts to strengthen the "sentimental bonds" forced him to fictionalize from his own memory. Transformations of experience were different. He concluded "writing is, I suppose a superstitious way of keeping the horror at bay, of keeping the evil outside."

For a dedicated smoker like Bowles, kif functioned as a passageway to enlightenment. He wrote solely in the physical world about Cannabis variations such as hashish and kif with tobacco that gave users a high degree of exoticism, alcohol-blurred vision, or contemplation and inaction with kif. Compare the risks from dedicated hashish and kif smoking shown by Bowles and Charles Baudelaire in *The Flowers of Evil* and *Artificial Paradise* where the "passageway" with both poems and pictures of sex and near-death are lined with spiritual perceptions that can only be seen as dreams and hallucinations.

Illustrations by Henry Chapront, *Les Paradis Artificiels (Opium et Haschisch)* by Charles Baudelaire. Paris: Société des Médecins Bibliophiles, 1921.

Bowles from the liner notes of the recording of *A Hundred Camels in the Courtyard*:

Moroccan kif-smokers like to speak of "two worlds," the one ruled by inexorable natural laws, and the other, the kif world, in which each person perceives "reality" according to the projections of his own essence, the state of consciousness in which the elements of the physical universe are automatically rearranged by Cannabis to suit the requirements of the individual. These distorted variations in themselves are of scant interest to anyone but the subject at the time he is experiencing them. An intelligent smoker, nevertheless, can aid in directing the process of deformation in such a way that the results will have value to him in his daily life. If he has faith in the accuracy of his interpretations, he will accept them as decisive, and use them to determine a subsequent plan of action. Thus, for a dedicated smoker, the passage to the "other world" is often a pilgrimage undertaken for the express purpose of oracular consultation.

In 1960 I began to experiment with the idea of constructing stories whose subject matter would consist of disparate elements and unrelated characters taken directly from life and fitted together as in a mosaic. The problem was to create a story line which would make each arbitrarily chosen episode compatible with the others, to make each one lead to the next with a semblance of naturalness. I believed that through the intermediary of kif the barriers separating the unrelated elements might be destroyed, and the disconnected episodes forced into a symbiotic relationship.

This constituted the bulk of the factual material I gave myself to work with.... No one of the actual situations had anything to do with kif, but by providing kif-directed motivations I was able to use Cannabis both as solvent and solder in the construction.

He of the Assembly has no factual anchors apart from three hermetic statements made to me that year by a kif-smoker in Marrakech: "The eye wants to sleep, but the head is no mattress," "The earth trembles and the sky is afraid, and the two eyes are not brothers," and "A pipe of kif before breakfast gives a man the strength of a hundred camels in the courtyard," He uttered these apocalyptic sentences, but steadfastly refused to shed any light on their meanings or possible applications. This impelled me to invent a story about him in which he would furnish the meanings....

— Paul Bowles

Paul Bowles Reads A Hundred Camels in the Courtyard. Number 68 of 100 limited edition LP recorded 1978 in Tangier, Morocco. Cover illustration: watercolour of the Djmaa el Fna by Brion Gysin from the collection of Am Here Books.

SUPPLEMENTAL ILLUSTRATIONS

The opposite engraving by Henry Sandham is from the title page of a 1884 book (*Lalla Rookh. An Oriental Romance*) filled with narrative poems, prose, and illustrations that are like a pictorial opera showing a larger-than-life motive force as the essence of the romance.[1] In this scene an angel is hovering over Lalla who is spread in an intoxicated position on the ottoman while holding a hookah. It is the same paralyzed position assumed by writer Mary C. Hungerford, a daily user of Indian hemp (hasheesh). She penned an article for *Popular Science Monthly* in 1882 and the magazine printed it again in 1884. The story tells of her experiences under the influence of Cannabis doses smoked and/or eaten. A caption for this illustration is used in a modern reprint of Hungerford's article *An Overdose of Hasheesh*.[2] There is no better caption than Hungerford's quote: "I died, as I believed, although by a strange double consciousness I knew that I should again reanimate the body I had left." The ghostly dissociated image of Lalla above Hungerford confirms her episode of double consciousness. The emphasis on the Spirit World in *Keef* suggests that the ghost was not accidental or deliberate. A mirror image engraving of the ghost was found in direct contact staining against the front of the page with no modern protective tissue paper. The reader may find a copy of that engraving on the next page and judge for themself.

At the very least, death-dreams and near-death visions are common with hashish and the potent Cannabis kif used by the hero and heroine in the present novel written by T.W. Coakley. Recent Cannabis studies have found convincing evidence for these so-called death-dreams and the underlying death cognitions.[3]

---

1 Book by Thomas Moore. Boston: Estes and Lauriat, 1888. Lalla Rookh or Lala-Rukh (Persian name meaning "tulip-cheeked") taken from the daughter of a seventeenth century emperor who was a heroine in a frame tale.

2 "An Overdose of Hasheesh" in *Sisters of the Extreme. Women Writing on The Drug Experience.* Edited by Cynthia Palmer and Michael Horowitz. Rochester, VT: Park Street Press, 1982; pp. 62–66.

3 Nagar, M. & S. Rabinovitz. "Smoke your troubles away: Exploring the effects of death cognitions on Cannabis craving and consumption." *Journal of Psychoactive Drugs*, Volume 47 (2), April – June 2015, pp. 91–99.

About This Illustration

The opposite engraving was credited to E.H. Garrett and used as the frontispiece for *Lalla Rookh. An Oriental Romance* written by Thomas Moore's first story published in 1817. This Lalla Rookh was created in 1884 shown smoking hashish from a hookah then paralyzed by visions of her dreams. The poetry and prose of Moore's text suggests a spiritual state and mentions other drugs. Compare her to the mirror image "ghost" stain on the previous page. Judge it as either accidental, deliberate, or a coincidence with the Spirit World.

Moore's poetry described Lalla's hope in dreams, scents of herbs, her flowerly crown, and "the visions that oft to worldly eyes." The stanza below is typical.

> The dream of the injured patient mind,
> That smiles at the wrongs of men,
> Is found in the bruised and wounded rind
> Of the cinnamon, sweetest then!
> Then hasten we, maid,
> To twine our braid,
> To-morrow the dreams and flowers will fade.

Lalla Rookh

ABOUT THIS ILLUSTRATION

The opposite illustration was painted by Austrian illustrator Gottfried Sieben (1856–1918) who was known for his popular subjects including caricatures and erotic drawings. This image appeared in *Haschisch: An Oriental Legend* (1898). In the story, Zuleyka falls in love with Ali and her father sends female jinns to seduce Ali with hashish. Here Ali is lying down with the tube from the skull-shaped hookah near his mouth. He sees death in the jingling clothes of a jester, a skeletal man with a rattling, bony hand and dying face. Ali dreams as he falls asleep with a blissful expression, pale face and painful tremors. The nude angel whispers "Hashish, hashish" and Ali wakes up. She tempts him to every new indulgence. He smoked then slept as reality mingled with phantoms of his dreams. Despite the angel's seductive magical power, death and strange fates beset him. The rest of the book takes him on an endless trip of true hallucinations. Years later Zuleyka finds Ali but is unable to save him:[1]

> Zuleyka knelt down next to Ali, lifted his head and gave him a kiss. He smiled blissfully, then gave a quiet sigh and he was no more. "The struggle is over, the suffering is over," she whispered. "Now you are truly well because adversaries and demons have no more power over you and a [heavenly] paradise of peace awaits you, my beloved in life and death!"

---

1 See *Hashish: The Lost Legend. The first English translation of a great oriental romance.* Edited by R.K. Siegel. Translations by Hermann Schibli (German) and Mindle Crystel Gross (Yiddish). Port Townsend, WA: Process Media and RKS Library Editions, 2013. [Illustration from page 40].

ABOUT THIS ILLUSTRATION

**Les Fumeurs de Hadchids
or Les Fumeurs de Kif**
The Smokers of Hashish or The Smokers of Kif
Lithograph from series by Gavarni, c. 1845

"Two men of the bourgeoisie enjoy their hashish pipes, their facial expressions evidence of their pleasant intoxication. Their dialogue, which is quite interesting, reveals the mental and physical effects of the drug, and runs as follows:

"Ah, I am beginning to experience oriental pleasure. . . I feel like I'm trotting on a camel's back! . . . And I, I think I just received a bastinado."

"Bastinado" is the European word for a form of punishment that was common in the East, especially Turkey and China, and consisted of blows to the feet with a bamboo stick. The term is humorously (masochistically?) used here, for the gentleman is undoubtedly referring to the physical effects of the drug, experienced as a tingling in his feet, the "bastinado," and referred to as an "oriental pleasure." The print is also of special interest as it is contemporary to the Club des Haschischins." [1]

---

1 French translations by William Dailey who permitted use of this work originally published in his antiquarian book catalog entitled *Phantastica*, 1979. Full catalog details are not listed here.

ENDPIECE

The ballet tells the story of an impossible love between a human and a spirit, especially seeing man's inherent temptation for the unknown and sometimes dangerous life. The same is true when the human falls in love in the spiritual world opened with the dreams of hashish or kif, either dreams of pleasure or death. Mary Hungerford showed us the obvious risks with overdoses of hashish. Ali lost his way with his wife Zuleyka and was trapped with death-dreams and visions confusing reality. Coakley told us the cause of life or death is always the pursuit of kif and love. Abecassis loses his spirit bride and goes home dying on the ship *La Sylphide* while the sylphs are carried to heaven in the ballet. Dancers en pointe gives them the appearance of being closer to the Spirit World. The dégagé or disengage is when a dancer moves their leg off the floor from a position of a pointed foot and straight leg moving or disengages. Filippo Tanglioni, the Italian choreographer of the seminal romantic ballet *La Sylphide* has succeeded as creator of dance steps to heaven.

Fairies From Taglioni's *La Sylphide* Returning To The Spirit World

ENDPIECE NOTES

At the core of *Keef* is an artist's memoir tracing his life from a joyful discovery of painting under the influence, through a Pygmalion infatuation with one of his portraits, then on to a final collapse that forces him to stop painting and begin dying. Coakley has given us a masterful literary look at the artist's journey from romance to tragedy. It is reminiscent of a modern talented artist, the late cartoonist Dave Sheridan, who excelled in providing a lighter view of a journey under the influence of Cannabis. In a series of sketches entitled *Stoned*, Sheridan's work illustrates the intoxicated mental states that Coakley described so well in words. Here he has given us his own frontispiece and endpiece for the journey in the Sixties (1960s).

Frontispiece · Endpiece

 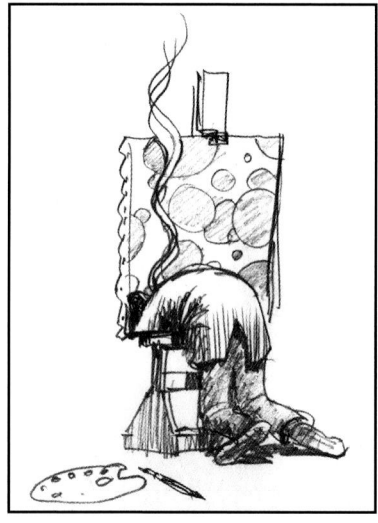

Artistically Stoned I · *Artistically Stoned II*

I have chosen to honor Coakley's book and keep the historical accuracy of this edition's illustrations by selecting a contemporary of his time, the French illustrator Gustave Fraipont, for the 1891 frontispiece and endpiece.

The frontispiece kif smoker heralds the story by posing as a Scheherazade-like character telling a never-ending tale from the *Arabian Nights*. The endpiece is a hashish dream from *La Sylphide* (1832), a romantic ballet of the supernatural by choreographer Filippo Taglioni. In the ballet a young man falls in love with a beautiful sylph, an imaginary spirit that takes the form of a forest fairy. As he embraces the sylph, her wings fall off, she shudders and dies. Her sister fairies carry her body aloft as the heartbroken man collapses. In *Keef*, the ship *La Sylphide* carries the dying Abecassis—who lost his "spirit bride"—back home to Tangiers where he dies.

As glimpsed through the fumes of smoke in the endpiece drawing by Fraipont, the fairies who danced on the stage of life end up in the spirit world. Perhaps everybody who died in the book ends up in the same spirit world when the book of life is closed. This might include Abecassis, Esther, Ralph Black, even Coakley. That would be a welcomed ending to this book, kindling our imagination about life in a spirit world filled with fairies and elves. Andreas Untersberger (1864–1933), Austrian artist of spiritual themes, gave us a glimpse of that life in *The Smoking Artist*:

RKS

ACKNOWLEDGMENTS

The novel *Keef* had its roots in nineteenth-century Morocco. This annotated and illustrated edition was built on a similar foundation for which I thank Jane Barack, my wife and thoughtful critic. She returned from a *Geographic* trip to Morocco and brought back the same sense of the excitement and magic that had attracted early travelers during the time of Coakley. From the crowded markets of Fez, through the busy streets of Marrakesh, she and her camel braved sandstorms in the Moroccan Desert to bring back a vintage flying carpet for the main floor of the RKS Library. In a very real sense it was on this magic carpet that the present book was constructed with Jane's love and support.

Among the books lining the shelves was my first copy of *Keef* acquired from William Dailey, antiquarian bookseller, scholar and guru of drug literature. Bill also supplied many of the reference books used for both the backstory and illustrations here. His commentaries, conversations and critical evaluations through the years were as valuable as the books themselves. I am grateful to Michael Horowitz, author, littérateur, and antiquarian bookseller (Flashback Books) for filling my shelves with helpful volumes and especially for his passionate encouragement to select *Keef* for production as a RKS Library Edition.

Stephen J. Gertz, antiquarian bookseller, author, and founding editor of the blog *Booktryst*, provided support, advice, and constructive criticism throughout the writing. Steve Gertz wrote an intriguing Foreword in historical education beginning with the Civil War and highlights of drug use by Louisa May Alcott and several best-selling authors throughout the ages. Gertz favors the term psychotropic, an early American erudite term for a drug that has an altering effect on the mind, usually referring to tranquilizers or hallucinogens. He shows how such psychotropic drugs became popular in the literature of the eighteenth and nineteenth centuries, and now are coming of age in 2016 with Cannabis and kif.

I thank many others who helped this project: Tom Pope for feedback and suggestions on the book design and illustrations; Eric A. Bye for timely translations; Peter Barack and Matt Fragner for consultations; Dr. Richard Hulquist for helpful conversations and assistance with library research; Ray Peoples of the USPS for his considerate and friendly hand-delivery of illustrations from around the globe; Leslie Arthur of William Reese and Company for graciously providing a scan of *The Oval Portrait* illustration; Dava Sheridan for kind permission to use *Artistically Stoned I* and *Artistically Stoned II* by the late Dave Sheridan; and Michael John Thompson, antiquarian bookseller, for locating the presentation copy of *Keef* inscribed to Michael Ward that is now in the RKS Library. The inscription is shown here on page 197 and the cover on page 41. Finally, a special pat on the head to Lulu, our Champion standard poodle, and my writing companion, for comfort and unconditional love. And thanks to Flower, our new standard poodle puppy who takes naps on my oversized reading chair only to awaken and follow me whenever I take a break to get a treat for both of us.

For assistance beyond the call of duty in helping to weave the book and extra-illustrations together, I am indebted to Philip March, Book Design Editor and Technology Consultant. It was only because of Philip's dedication and craftsmanship that we were able to inject a "life likeness" into *Keef*, thereby resuscitating a lost and forgotten masterpiece.

THE END

RKS Library Editions is dedicated to the rescue and resurrection of lost and forgotten masterpieces of drug literature. Titles are chosen for their literary value, historical importance, intriguing backstory, original illustrations, and scarcity. All books are initially published as deluxe limited editions in their original format, translated into English if necessary, and provided with historical notes, annotations and extra-illustrations from the RKS Library Collection. Our motto is: "Once lost and forgotten, now found and unforgettable." The Editorial Board and Contributors consist of world-renowned antiquarian authorities, authors, collectors, booksellers and experts in the genre.